How To Create A Depression-Free Life

By Marie O'Neil, D.B.S.
Depression-Busting Specialist

By Marie O'Neil
Copyright © 2017 Mirdad Ltd.
All Rights Reserved Worldwide.
Second Edition. First Published 2017.
ISBN-13: 978-1548238162
ISBN-10: 1548238163

ACKNOWLEDGEMENTS

Diana - Much love and thanks for your continued support, love and encouragement throughout this entire project and in my life. Your open heart and generous spirit is an inspiration to me. Thank you for your precious friendship. Big hugs xxx

Michelle - Thank you for being a beautiful sister. Without your creative inspiration, I wouldn't be who I am today. Thank you for being you. Love you always xxx

Mum - Without your love and unwavering support (even in times, I'm suffering from creative frustration, and am therefore, impossible to deal with), this book would never have been completed. Thank you for being, not just my mother, but my best friend. Love you forever xxx

How To Create A Depression-Free Life

By Marie O'Neil, D.B.S.

Depression-Busting Specialist

CONTENTS

	Acknowledgements	iii
	Introduction	1
	SECTION ONE **How To Free Your Mind From Depression**	9
1	Let's Look At Depression Differently	11
2	**The First Depression-Causing Layer**	17
3	Let's Dissolve The First Depression-Causing Layer	23
4	Pulled In Every Direction?	28
5	**The Second Depression-Causing Layer**	32
6	Why We Do, What We Do?	37
7	Missing Out On The Life You Were Meant To Have?	56
8	Are We Mistaken About Mistakes?	60
9	**The Third Depression-Causing Layer**	66
10	Feel You're Not Good Enough?	70
11	You Are The Prize!	78
12	The True Journey of Life	80
	SECTION TWO **How To Free Your Body From Depression**	85
13	How You Feel, Matters!	87
14	Groundbreaking Science Shouts 'STOP!' – Will You Listen?	96

SECTION THREE - Practical Resources: Transform Your Emotions And Your Life   115

15	Don't Just Prune The Leaves!	117
16	Experiencing Great Sadness?	125
17	Experiencing Great Anger?	129
18	Instant Tranquillizer + Rapid De-Stress Technique	134
19	11 Minutes To Inner Calm And Tranquility	138
20	Experience The *'Gap'*	141
21	Happiness Starts With An Inner Smile	145
22	Just Say *'Yes'*	147

SECTION FOUR Create Your Depression-Free Future   151

23	Your Depression-Free Life Requires Attention	153

Your Essential Companion   165

24	The Create A Depression-Free Life Show	167
25	About The Author	169

INTRODUCTION

Would you like to free yourself from depression but nothing seems to work?

If you're nodding 'yes', then you're in the right place, at the right time and you're going to love what I'm about to share with you.

You are moments away from discovering the THREE MAJOR DRIVERS which can thrust all of us into depression, no matter our age, sex, culture, walk of life or religion.

I prefer to call these drivers: *Layers.* As they have a way of wrapping themselves around us, entombing us in their thick, heavy, unyielding darkness. One which is near impossible to break-free from. Unless you know how and soon you will.

- Imagine if you knew with complete confidence that depression was just a thing of your past, not your future?

- Imagine finally discovering how to rip depression right out by the roots? How great would that feel, *knowing* that like an uprooted tree, it could never grow back?

- Imagine all the things you could make happen in your career, your relationships, with your body, your health, your wealth, and throughout your entire life, if you were totally freed from the toxic condition of depression?

Now, you may be thinking; *"Yes! That sounds great but I've heard all these grand promises before and nothing has worked for me in the past. So why would this be any different?"*

And, that's a great question!

Why should you listen to me and why is this book so different, from the millions of other self-help books on the market today?

Fortunately, the answer is simple.

This book is the only one of its kind. Seriously, shop around! I guarantee you won't find another book which pinpoints the EXACT THREE MAJOR DRIVERS of depression, like this one does. None.

They all just give you vague ideas. They simply say such things as: *"You must change your beliefs, to change your life."*

But, here's what they don't tell you.

Those beliefs they're insisting you change, are buried so deep in your subconscious mind, you cannot find them on your own.

In fact, have you ever said: *"I just don't know why I do what I do?"*

Well, you're not alone because that's our subconscious thoughts and beliefs driving our external behaviour. So, unless you have magical powers and can *instantly pinpoint* the exact beliefs which are driving your depression, you're facing a losing battle.

You know, it's hard enough dealing with depression itself without, having to worry about *"which"* belief is the right one to change, to change your life.

But, you can rest assured.

As I've said, *this book accurately identifies the exact beliefs which drive depression* within all of us, no matter our age, sex, culture, walk of life or religion.

Now, I didn't just *'stumble'* across these depression-causing beliefs. Nor did I conjure up all the valuable tips, tools, practical solutions and *little-known* techniques held within the pages of this book, overnight.

Far from it!

In fact, what most people who meet me today don't know, is I haven't always been the confident, self-assured, positive, 39-year-old woman I am today. No. The truth is, over 12 years ago I was suicidal and in the depths of depression. And, I was so desperate to get away from the excruciating pain of depression that I was willing, to drive a 44 tonne, truck and trailer unit off the side of the highway, to get some relief from the torment, the pain, the all-consuming intensity of depression.

I used to say to myself: *"Nobody will miss me if I'm gone!" "Nobody cares!" "I'm useless!" "A failure!" "I have no value in this world, so what's the point me being here?!"*

It's a place that mere words cannot describe and nobody, but those who have stood in that place and faced that intense darkness head-on, could ever understand.

Now, what stopped me from taking the plunge and driving my 44 tonne truck and trailer unit off the highway, that fateful night?

Well, in a weird twist of fate, my depression saved me! You see, I had an overwhelming belief that if I drove off the road, I'd screw that up too! Just like I'd screwed everything else up in my life, at that time.

And, as if that constant daily turmoil wasn't struggle enough!

I read some scientific studies which showed that a shocking 50% of those who recover from one episode of depression, had one or more additional episodes throughout their lifetime, and approximately 80% of those with two episodes had another recurrence. *(American Psychiatric Association, 2000; Kupfer, Frank, & Wamhoff, 1996; Post, 1992).*

I didn't like those odds! In fact, *I couldn't afford* for those statistics to be true. My life depended on it.

So, I began to question, could these shocking statistics be true?

The unfortunate truth is yes, and I'll tell you why.

In over a decade of thorough and at times, painstaking research, I discovered that **most depression treatments simply deal with the symptoms and not the cause.** They treat our irregular sleeping patterns, our angry or sadness, but they do not tend to what is truly driving depression itself. They do not attack depression from the roots up. They do not destroy what's *breathing life* into our emotional outbursts, feelings of hopelessness or erratic behaviour!

Therefore, it's natural we would always have recurrent bouts of depression, because we're attempting to kill the tree, by simply chopping its branches. All the while, leaving the roots in the ground for it to grow back stronger.

And, here's the truth...

The more we experience depression, the more we feel defeated by it and the more we believe it's an unconquerable enemy. However, the reality is, it can be defeated if only, we destroy it from the roots up. The choice is ours.

Today, you are standing in the very same place I stood over 12 years ago. In the depths of depression and faced with just three options.

1. The First Option: You can give up on your hopes, dreams and that future you've secretly dreamt about. Give up on getting out of depression and keep doing what you're doing. **But, let's be honest...You wouldn't have read up to this point, if you wanted that.** You're here because you *know* you deserve a better life.

2. The Second Option: You can go it alone and just like me, you can wrestle and struggle your way out of depression, without a torch to guide you through the darkness. I'll be blunt, it's very tough, mentally draining, exhausting, excruciatingly painful and not to mention, time-consuming without the shortcuts I now know. However, it can be done and this is the option for people, who are strong in studying complex psychological, emotional and behavioural concepts, wading through mountains of statistical data, scientific papers and other related theories or materials.

3. The Third Option: Is to simply read this book from cover to cover, absorb all the valuable depression-crushing insights and then integrate them into your life, so you can see and feel the results, just as I have.

Now, you may be asking: *"What am I going to discover in this book that I can't learn anywhere else?"*

Another great question! So, let me explain what you'll discover.

This depression-busting book is split into four user-friendly sections.

The first section is called: **How To Free Your Mind From Depression.** This is where we dive straight into the three major *layers* and associated beliefs which drive depression.

No longer will you have to painstakingly deep-dive into your subconscious for weeks, months or even years, searching for *that one magical belief* which is driving all your troubles because I've done all the hard work for you. That's right!

After you complete this section, there will be <u>no more guesswork</u> when it comes to what's driving your self-defeating thoughts and behaviour. You will know.

You will also be armed with the vital knowledge to transform and eliminate these *depression-causing* mindsets, starting today!

Next, we leap into section two which is called: **How To Free Your Body From Depression.**

Did you know that the common advice of exercising our way out of depression, can actually drive you deeper into depression? Sounds strange I know. Since, all the typical evidence seems to suggest otherwise.

However, leading scientific research shows exercise may NOT be the answer at all.

So, what is?

Well, that's exactly what you're going to discover throughout this section. How to correctly approach depression to rapidly *alleviate the causes* driving many of the common symptoms, such as; irrational crying, angry outbursts, low self-esteem, inability to focus or complete day-to-day tasks, among many others.

You'll also be armed with vital scientific insights, regarding a very natural chemical and biological process which occurs within each and every one of us.

Why is this vital to know?

Because when this natural process is disturbed, it quite literally **throws us into a depressed state**. *(mentally, emotionally and physically)*. Which is not what you want. You don't want to *just* rid yourself of depression today, you also want to protect yourself from it ever returning.

So, for that very reason, I'm going to take you by the hand and guide you through simple, yet powerful strategies to take charge of your chemicals and ultimately, your life (no, it's got nothing to do with exercising, socialising or eating the right foods). This is a brand-new approach and therefore, will help you reap brand-new results.

Truth is, this one section will turn much of what you've been taught about depression, on its head!

But hey! As the saying goes, if you do what you've always done, you'll get what you've always got. So, if you want different results and you want to radically transform your mindset, emotional well-being and your life, you've got to do something different. This section will show you how.

The third section is the Practical Resources Section. Now, don't be fooled! This is not just more of the same-old repackaged advice for treating depression. As I've already said, this book is second to none. So naturally, this section is packed with the latest, proven techniques to alleviate depression.

You will discover a wealth of knowledge which will give you a fresh, new approach to depression and many of its symptoms.

If you're wanting long-lasting relief from depression, you can't go wrong by implementing the valuable tips and step-by-step techniques held within this information-packed section.

And the fourth and final section, is where we step into the world of quantum physics to discover *how* you can rapidly create your very own depression-free life, starting today. That's right! We leave fluffy, whimsical theories at the door and take a deep-dive into the science of how you can create the happiest, most fulfilling life you could ever imagine.

Does all this sound too good to be true?

Well, I used to think so too, until I implemented these strategies into my own life and saw some powerful results.

So, are you ready?

Are you ready to say *'yes'* to creating your depression-free future, starting today?

Well, let's get started because there's no time to waste.

Marie O'Neil

Depression-Busting Specialist
Author, Speaker, Life Coach
Creator of: Create A Depression-Free Life Show
Facebook: @MarieONeilOfficial
www.CreateADepressionFreeLife.com

SECTION 1

HOW TO FREE YOUR MIND FROM DEPRESSION

1

LET'S LOOK AT DEPRESSION DIFFERENTLY

To get out of depression we must work SMARTER, not harder. After all, who has the energy to work harder to get out of depression? I know I didn't. So, unlike the usual depression advice out there, I'm NOT going to ask you to *'think more positively'* or force some unnatural change on yourself. In fact, I don't want you to stress about changing anything at all.

Instead, I ask you to simply sit back, relax, put your feet up, soak in all the insightful words on the following pages and discover that you're already beautiful just the way you are and you don't require any improvement whatsoever. Which may raise the question...

So why am I stuck in the depths of depression then?

Well, to discover the answer to that question we must turn to the 16th century, to the great renaissance artist Michelangelo and his statue of David which he completed in 1504.

11

Image: Michelangelo's Statue of David

When asked how he created such a fine sculpture, Michelangelo declared that he never *created* his infamous masterpiece of David at all. All he did, was simply *unlock* David from the block of marble which had encased him all those long arduous years. To Michelangelo, David was always there inside that specific block of marble the whole time. From Michelangelo's eyes, his exquisite masterpiece of David was never created out of marble but rather *freed* from it.

Don't you agree this is such a beautiful tale? Not only does it speak of how creative souls see this beautiful world around us but it also **speaks an absolute truth to every one of us suffering in depression**, if we're open to hear it.

Reality is, each one of us has a pristine and very beautiful masterpiece locked away, deep inside of us, which is just *waiting to be released from the excess layers* surrounding it. However, unlike David, whose layers were made from marble, our *'layers'* are made from:

- Society's expectations
- Family expectations
- Duties

- Beliefs
- Value systems
- Honour codes
- Religions
- Educational systems
- Pecking orders
- Definitions of right and wrong
- What's beautiful versus what's defined as ugly
- And the list goes on......

THE TRUE MEANING OF DEPRESSION

Have you ever looked at the true meaning of the word depression? It comes from the Latin word *dēprimere* which means to press down, lower (de-press), or to repress.

In other words, **<u>de-pression is a state</u>** in which the beautiful masterpiece of YOU is being repressed.

Your true self is being de-pressed and you're suffocating behind layers of society, in the very same way the masterpiece of David, was suffocating all those long arduous years entombed beneath layers of marble.

Take a moment to ask yourself:

➤ Are there any parts of yourself you're currently pushing down or repressing?

➤ Are there parts of yourself you're afraid to show to others?

➤ Are there parts of yourself you're ashamed of?

➤ Do you feel the *'real you'* isn't good enough?

➤ Do you have an irrational fear of rejection?

These are all common signs that we're hiding our exquisite masterpiece (our true selves) from the world, which is **unknowingly holding us hostage in the depths, darkness and distress of depression**.

But how does this occur?

Well, as a child we came into this world helpless, we needed others for our survival. So, from day one, others told us how to think, how to feel, how to respond, how to act and how to see the world around us. As a result, we became entombed within layers upon layers of thoughts, feelings, beliefs and emotions which didn't even belong to us. Our real self, got *pushed down, depressed and buried out of sight*.

This is the exact reason why we feel so lost in depression. We have quite literally lost touch with who we naturally are, our true essence. It's as if we've been kidnapped from our comfortable home and taken to a cold, damp, dark place. A place we have no idea how to escape from, simply because we have no idea where we are. We've lost all sense of direction and therefore, have no idea how to get back home. We are lost.

Therefore, it's very difficult to discern what's right or wrong, or even which way is up in depression. Nothing makes sense, simply because we've lost touch with our true compass bearings, our North Star, our own voice, our own centre.

Why do you think depression is such a dark space?

We're literally *buried alive* in layers upon layers of *'societal dirt'*, which blocks out all light and entombs us in complete darkness.

I don't know about you but I always felt depression to be an extremely claustrophobic, dark place where it was hard to breathe. Sometimes I felt trapped. Other times, I felt I was drowning in the depths. However, the moment we recognise we're buried, repressed, depressed under such heavy societal layers, it makes sense that we'd feel this way.

The great news is, unlike David, you don't have to wait and hope for a master craftsman like Michelangelo to come along and *chip away* all those excess layers to set you free, you can do it yourself.

That's right!

Throughout this book you're going to **discover everything you need to know** to set the exquisite *'Masterpiece of YOU'* free.

You can finally bust out of all those restrictive and claustrophobic layers, which are causing you to feel constricted, small, depressed, anxious, indecisive, unconfident, lacking in self-esteem and leaving you unable to live life to the fullest.

Do you want to know the best part?

After hundreds of hours of sleepless nights, thousands of dollars spent on workshops and over 19 years of sometimes, extremely arduous research, I discovered that at the heart of every issue, every problem, every conflict, every anxiety, every depressed moment, every fear, were just **Three Destructive, Life-Sapping Depression-Causing Layers**.

That's right! There's just three toxic layers currently burying and enshrouding your pristine masterpiece in darkness.

The Three Toxic Depression-Causing Layers

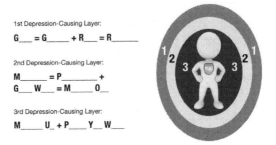

1st Depression-Causing Layer:

G____ = G_____ + R____ = R_____

2nd Depression-Causing Layer:

M_____ = P_____ +
G___ W___ = M_____ 0__

3rd Depression-Causing Layer:

M_____ U_ + P_____ Y___ W____

It's these very layers which are causing you to suffocate under their weight. Keeping you stuck in the vicious cycle of depression and forcing you to live a life far less than you desire and deserve.

So, are you ready to say **'yes'** to tearing down all three hideous, soul-destroying, depression-causing layers as fast as possible, so you can **start walking into a depression-free future?**

Well, let's get started because there's no time to waste!

2

THE FIRST DEPRESSION-CAUSING LAYER

The first outer-most layer of the three extremely harmful depression-causing layers which currently surround the beautiful *Masterpiece of YOU,* is the layer of: **Good = Getting + Right = Rewards**.

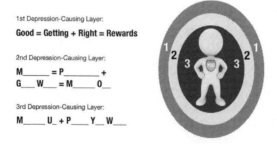

1st Depression-Causing Layer:

Good = Getting + Right = Rewards

2nd Depression-Causing Layer:

M_____ = P_____ +
G___ W___ = M_____ O__

3rd Depression-Causing Layer:

M_____ U_ + P_____ Y__ W____

    To understand how this happiness-destroying layer keeps us locked in the intense darkness of depression, we must take a quick journey back to our childhood.

    Can you remember hearing a version of the following phrases when you were growing up?

- *If you behave, you'll get a treat.*
- *If you eat all the greens on your plate, you can have dessert.*
- *If you wash the dishes, you can stay up and watch a movie.*
- *If you do your homework, you can go to your friend's house.*
- *If you complete your chores, you can go and play outside.*
- *If you behave, your treat will be that you don't get a kick up the butt!*

I'm positive we can all recall similar scenarios from our childhood, no matter which corner of the globe we reside in. But what did these seemingly innocent scenarios teach our very young and impressionable minds?

They taught us, that in life **if we're good, we'll get and if we act right, we'll be rewarded** (or at the very least, we'll avoid punishment).

Not only did our family's, our educational systems, our religious doctrines and society, all teach us variations of this very same message: *Good = Getting + Right = Rewards* but they also employed a very unsuspecting celebrity to jump on the same brainwashing bandwagon.

Can you think of who it is?

He's so cuddly and friendly you'd probably never suspect him but for over 80 years he's been **strengthening and tightening this extremely harmful, depression-causing layer** of: Good = Getting + Right = Rewards around us. He's driven this message into the majority of homes in the Western World.

Can you guess who he is? Let me give you a clue...

He's making a list,

He's checking it twice,
He's gonna find out who's naughty or nice
Santa Claus is coming to town
He sees you when you're sleeping
And he knows when you're awake
He knows if you've been bad or good
So be good for goodness sake!

(Song: Santa Claus Is Comin' to Town. Written by John Frederick Coots and Haven Gillespie and was first sung in November 1934).

Yes! It's the infamous Santa Claus who helped drive this message of:

- GOOD (being good, doing good, getting good grades, a good job, etc.) EQUALS GETTING

- RIGHT (being right, doing the right thing, behaving right, etc.) EQUALS REWARDS

In fact, in the very same way the slow creeping, unsuspecting ivy engulfs anything within its strangling vines, this unsuspecting layer ever-so slowly engulfs our pristine masterpiece, little by little, suffocating us, until one day, BOOM! Our priceless masterpiece is entirely enshrouded in a veil of darkness. A thick poisonous mind-altering layer which permeates every area of our lives, without us even knowing it.

Have you ever had that nagging feeling that something is missing in your life?

It is! Your connection to the very source of YOU, your true self (your masterpiece) and when we're disconnected from ourselves, we're disconnected from life itself. And whilst we continue to keep our true selves (our masterpiece) locked up inside, we'll continue to stay in a state of de-pression.

Therefore, the key to releasing ourselves from the clutches of depression, is not found outside of ourselves, it's found within us.

But how do we know whether this first detrimental layer of: *Good = Getting + Right = Rewards* is currently affecting our lives and driving us deeper into depression?

Ask yourself:

- Do you ever complain when bad things happen to good people?
  Be aware these thoughts and feelings only arise within us, if we believe that being or doing good is rewarded. It's the very same principle that many religions base their version of the *'only the righteous go to heaven'* statement on.

- Do you constantly feel compelled to impress others?
  In other words, you're not relaxed and natural in the presence of others. You have a deep-seated fear of rejection or not fitting in. You may constantly think about what's the right thing to do, or how to get others to like (or accept) you, etc.

- Do you obsess about looking good or nice in the eyes of others?
  Note: The definition of looking good in the eyes of others is purely dependent upon our environments. What's seen as good and therefore, rewarded in one environment, may not be in another. For example: In one environment, being good is achieving straight A's or 100% in everything they do and not a percentile less. In another environment, being good is successfully stealing a car or robbing a bank. So, don't get locked into thinking good only means a *'goody two shoes'* type of good.

- Are you pursuing a career, a lifestyle choice, a relationship status, etc., simply because others expect it from you or because you believe it raises your status in the eyes of others?

- Do you refuse to speak up or *'rock the boat'* because you prefer to stay in everyone's good books?

- Do you believe if you do all the right things, tick all the right boxes, you'll stay on the right track and everything will work out perfectly for you? Or at the very least, it'll be smooth sailing?

- Do you believe the right path/track has less bumps, bad times, struggles or hazards than the so-called wrong path/track?

- Do you believe if you fall in love with the right person, you will have very little or no disagreements, the both of you will just gel and you'll live happily ever after?

- Do you believe hard work automatically entitles you to the prize, a reward, approval or that pat on the back?

- Do you believe if you just act the right way, dress the right way and say all the right things, your date will be a success or your relationship will go the way you want? In other words, you'll get the right result.

These are just a mere glimpse at some of the common mindsets which are naturally born out of this harmful and very toxic first layer of: *Good = Getting + Right = Rewards*.

We must be aware that the longer we stay wrapped up and confined within this first harmful layer, the longer we'll experience these common thought-processes and unknowingly, drive ourselves deeper into the never-ending downward spiral of depression.

So, what's the solution?

How do we tear down this layer completely so we can free ourselves and walk into a depression-free future?

Well that's exactly what we're going to be discussing in the next chapter, so I'll see you there!

3

LET'S DISSOLVE THE FIRST
DEPRESSION-CAUSING LAYER

We've just discovered the first, outer-most layer of:
Good = Getting + Right = Rewards which is
currently enshrouding the *Masterpiece of YOU* in total
darkness, keeping you locked in the cycle of depression.
Therefore, it's now time to check out some straight-
forward, practical solutions to rapidly tear down this
first, outermost layer.

The first step, is to take a few moments and answer
what I like to call **The Five Questions to
Authenticity**.

These five questions will gently, but very rapidly,
start dissolving this outer layer by allowing you to move
closer to and uncover the true essence of who you are
(your exquisite masterpiece).

Be aware, the faster you re-discover your true self
and bring your masterpiece back out into the light again,
the faster you'll catapult yourself out of the darkness of

depression.   Your true essence will no longer be repressed or *de-pressed* in an unhealthy state of being.

Remember, even though much of the usual advice instructs us to change ourselves, to get out of depression, the essence of this book and the intention behind my words is NOT about changing you, or turning you into something you're not. It's about uncovering the beauty that you already are. The beauty you've forgotten to see. It's about uncovering the exquisite *Masterpiece of YOU* and naturally lifting you upwards, out of the clutches of depression.

The Five Questions to Authenticity

1. What have you done (or not done) because others expected or demanded it from you?

   For example: Have you followed a specific career path, married a certain person or stayed in a specific location to appease the wishes of others? Or have you NOT followed a specific career path, lifestyle choice, married a certain person or stayed in a specific location to appease the wishes of others?

2. What have you done (or not done) because you believed others expected or demanded it from you?

   This is when we do something simply because we *presume* it's what others want from us. However, we never stop and check to see if our presumptions are correct.

3. What have you done (or not done) because you believed it would make you look better in the eyes of others?

   In other words, what are you doing (or not doing) to get the *tick of approval* amongst your friends, family, colleagues, employers, sporting, religious, spiritual, interest groups, etc.

The answers we give to the above questions are things we're simply doing for others approval. So, take a moment right now to ponder all the ways you can start dropping these inauthentic activities or ways of being.

Ask yourself, **what steps can I take today to start moving closer towards my authentic self?**

What things can you drop to align yourself with your true essence, your true spirit? For example: What things are you currently doing just to *please others* but they fail to uplift your spirit or align with what feels right for you?

Whether we're aware of it or not, a major challenge we have whilst being stuck in depression is being terribly afraid to step up and be ourselves. We fear it with every cell in our being. Simply because we feel we're not accepted for being who we naturally are. We feel we must do things to be accepted or become a *'somebody'* to have any value.

Naturally, we're going to delve deeper into these thoughts and feelings in a later chapter but for now, start taking an honest look at your life and begin separating what you're doing because it **feels right for you** versus, what you're doing simply to be seen in a positive light by others (in other words, to belong, fit in, to secure that relationship, to not rock the boat or to get the tick of approval).

Then, move on to question four...

4. What things would you be doing today, if you were confident it didn't matter how you looked in the eyes of others?

    In other words, what activities would you try? What career or job path would you pursue? What interests or hobbies would you love to have a go at? Who would you date? Who would you hang out with? What chances would you take, if you didn't have any fear of rejection, looking foolish, falling short of expectations or failing?

5. What steps (no matter how small) can you take today to start moving into alignment with the more authentic part of yourself?

In other words, how can you begin putting into action the answers you gave to question four. For example: Are there groups you can join with your same interests or passions? Are there people you need to reduce or increase contact with? Are there situations you need to start saying *'no'* to, to start implementing personal boundaries, building your confidence and self-respect. Are there situations you need to start saying *'yes'* to, in order to; grow in new ways, open yourself up to new possibilities or drop the old status quo? Were there creative activities you did as a child that gave you immense enjoyment? Why not try them again now to reconnect and rediscover what makes your happiness soar?

Remember, when we've lost touch with ourselves for so many years, we must *re-learn* what excites us, what motivates us and what lifts our spirit once again, so explore all possibilities.

Start saying *'yes'* to new ideas, just to test what's helpful in bringing the beautiful *'Masterpiece of YOU'* back out into the light of day, once again.

Don't be afraid to try new things, as it's the only way to *'shake off'* all those hideous layers which have you currently entombed within the darkness of depression.

The faster you peel back all the layers to reveal your authentic wants, drives, hopes, dreams and desires that currently lie repressed (de-pressed) and out of sight, the faster you can drop this layer of: *Good = Getting + Right = Rewards* which suffocates you and sucks all the pleasure out of your life. Only then can you start to focus on what really and truly matters in life, which is:

What makes YOUR heart sing and YOUR mind come alive?

Now, I highly recommend completing these **Five Questions to Authenticity** <u>before</u> you skip ahead to the next chapter where we tap into some insightful ancient wisdom and I'm talking over 2,581 years old *'ancient'*. So, it's some real, authentic *'old-school'* wisdom which we can employ to move more rapidly towards a depression-free future.

See you there!

4

PULLED IN EVERY DIRECTION?

When we stand back and have a good honest look at this layer of: *Good = Getting + Right = Rewards*, we can instantly see that the root cause behind what's driving us to stay locked within it clutches, is **caring about the opinions of others** too much.

<u>We allow others to dictate</u> what is right and wrong for us.

When we're wrapped up in this layer, we live *via* the choices of others, and not our own. Again, this causes a repression of our being, we're de-pressing our true selves, our masterpiece. Which will lead us to live a life, far less than our fullest potential, not to mention, keep us stuck in the depths of depression.

This is the very reason I want to share a very beautiful, ancient fable from around the 5th century BC. The ancient wisdom contained within this simple, yet highly insightful fable, helps to re-focus our minds when we're not only trapped inside the tumultuous cycle of depression but also when we're being suffocated by this hideous layer of: *Good = Getting + Right = Rewards*.

The ancient fable goes something like this...

An old man and his young son are travelling with their donkey. As all three gently stroll along the road, side by side, a farmer passes them and says, *'you fool's, what is a donkey for but to ride upon?'* Listening to this farmer, the old man puts his son on the donkey and they carry on their journey.

It's not long before they pass a group of men, one of whom says to the group, *'see that lazy youngster, he lets his father walk whilst he rides.'* Overhearing these comments, the old man begins to feel uncomfortable, so he immediately orders his son off the donkey and gets on himself.

They don't get very far when they pass two women, one of whom says to the other, *'shame on that lazy old man for letting his poor little son trudge along behind whilst he sits on the donkey.'* Now, the old man doesn't know what to do. *'Ahhh, there's only one solution,'* he declares. They should both ride on the donkey. So, the old man helps his young son climb onto the donkey and they continue their journey.

As they come closer to the village they want to stay in, passersby begin to jeer and point at them. The old man instantly stops the donkey and asks the villagers what they have an issue with. One villager says, *'aren't you ashamed of yourself for overloading that poor donkey with yourself and your son? The poor donkey is dying! It would make more sense for you to carry the donkey.'*

Since they had almost reached the boundary of the village they were visiting, the old man felt it would be best to listen to the villagers, as he didn't want to look foolish or offend any of them. So, he cut down a pole, tied the donkey's feet to it and he and his son continue their journey carrying the donkey between their shoulders.

As you can imagine, the villagers start gathering, laughing, pointing and shouting, *'look at those fools! We have never seen such stupidity! A donkey is for riding upon not for being carried on your shoulders.'*

At that moment, the old man and his son begin to walk across a small bridge over a high canyon. This causes the upside-down donkey to instantly become terrified. He starts kicking recklessly to break free from his ropes. The donkey succeeds. However, the moment he frees himself, he plummets into the river below. The donkey instantly dies from the fall.

'That will teach you,' said a wise old man who had been following the pair from the very beginning of their journey. *'Just like that donkey, you will be dead if you continue to listen to people too much. Don't be affected by what others have to say, because there are as many opinions in this world as there are people. If you try to PLEASE ALL, YOU WILL PLEASE NONE.'*

(Credit: The Man, the Boy and the Donkey by Aesop circa. 620 – 564 BCE)

This beautiful tale shows us that we all have **two choices in life**:

1. We can continue to live within this depression-causing, anxiety-riddled, people-pleasing layer of *Good = Getting + Right = Rewards* and be continuously dragged in conflicting directions all in an attempt, to achieve the impossible which is to please everyone we meet. Or,

2. We can immediately tear down this layer, forget about fitting in or pleasing others' expectations of us and **start accepting ourselves just as we are and start doing what feels right for us**.

Now, this <u>does not</u> mean we turn into a complete selfish a**hole who doesn't give a damn about others. No, it doesn't mean that at all. What it DOES mean however, is that we need to start asking ourselves (at all times, until it becomes ingrained and second nature):

➢ Does this feel right for me? Or,

➢ Am I simply doing it, to fit in or please others?

From today, start feeling comfortable with saying 'NO' to others and 'YES' to yourself.

Remember this is YOUR life to live.

So, ask yourself, how do you want to live YOUR life? Via your choices? Or the choices of others? Do you want to direct your own course? Or have it directed by others?

Starting today:

✓ Bust-free from society's depression-causing layers.

✓ Be who YOU want to be.

✓ Live courageously and in a way, that fulfils YOUR heart.

Always remember, you are beautiful and you know what is right for you, you simply need to trust yourself.

So, why not start trusting yourself today?

I look forward to seeing you in the next chapter where we uncover the second, highly-detrimental, depression-causing layer. See you there!

5

THE SECOND DEPRESSION-CAUSING LAYER

As promised, in this chapter we're going to move inwards and delve deeper into the second, most harmful, depression-causing layer which helps to enshroud the exquisite, highly valuable *Masterpiece of YOU* in darkness. This second layer is the layer of: **Mistakes = Punishment + Going Wrong = Missing Out.**

1st Depression-Causing Layer:

Good = Getting + Right = Rewards

2nd Depression-Causing Layer:

Mistakes = Punishment + Going Wrong = Missing Out

3rd Depression-Causing Layer:

M_____ U_ + P____ Y__ W___

Can you remember a time in your childhood when you made a mistake or did the so-called *wrong thing* in the eyes of others? Can you recall what happened?

I can pretty much guarantee, if you're anything like me and you grew up in the early 80's or before, you most probably experienced a kick up the butt, you were grounded, or both.

We usually *missed out* on going to our friend's house or something we wanted to do, didn't we? We got sent to our bedroom or we had something we enjoyed playing with, taken away or withdrawn from us.

No matter which form it took, we can be sure, it always resulted in us being *punished or missing out* on something.

These natural childhood experiences unknowingly conditioned us to believe that in life: **Mistakes = Punishment + Going Wrong = Missing Out.** Hence, this second depression-causing layer was born.

You may have already recognised, this is where our deep-seated fear of *going wrong*, ending up on the *wrong track* in life, making *mistakes*, saying or doing the *wrong thing* is driven from. The roots of these depression-causing thoughts and feelings are all born from this second, much deeper layer of: *Mistakes = Punishment + Going Wrong = Missing Out*, which enshrouds our pristine masterpiece in yet another veil of mind-altering illusion.

How do you know if this layer of: **Mistakes = Punishment + Going Wrong = Missing Out** is currently suffocating the *Masterpiece of YOU*, keeping you locked in the downward spiral of depression?

Ask yourself:

- Do you feel it's okay to withdraw things from others when they don't do what you want, or what you expected them to do?
  This could be in the form of withdrawing your attention, your intimacy and affection, your support, your money, your communication, etc. You withdraw something, simply because somebody has not acted in a way you expected or even demanded.

- Do you feel excessively guilty when others withdraw things from you?
  In other words, does the *missing out* feeling and the associated punishment, make you feel bad about yourself or less valuable inside? Does it make you feel small and insignificant?

- Do you believe you can be punished for past mistakes, wrong choices or *'sins'*?

- When things in life don't turn out as you expected, do you either:
  - Punish and berate yourself for making a mistake or doing the so-called wrong thing, making the wrong choice or taking the wrong action. In other words, you chastise yourself for *being wrong* in some way, shape or form. Or do you,
  - Punish and berate others for their so-called mistakes or wrong doings, which you feel are causing you to suffer. In other words, *it's their fault* you're currently missing out or suffering in life.

- Are you constantly anxious about making a decision (even the simplest) out of fear of going wrong?

- Do you have an extreme fear of making mistakes in life?

- Do you get paralysed by all the *'what ifs'* that run through your mind?

- Do you frequently beat yourself up with all those happiness-depleting *'should've known better'* or *'if only'* type statements?

- Do you believe that one mistake, one wrong choice, one wrong decision or one wrong action can swiftly catapult you onto the wrong path or track in life?

- Do you believe it's possible for you to *miss out* on the life you were meant to have, if you take a wrong fork in the road?

If you have (or have ever had) any of the above thoughts or feelings, please don't be hard on yourself, or think there's anything wrong with you, or your mind. It's completely natural for us to think along these lines, especially when we've been entombed within these various depression-causing layers for so many years.

They've created a *smoke-screen* around us and completely distorted our personal view of ourselves, our inner value, reality and the world around us.

Therefore, it's vital for us to tear down all three layers, one by one, so we can begin to move closer and closer to our true essence, our true beauty and regain our natural clarity of mind, once again.

In fact, destroying all three layers is the only way to tap into the huge well of calmness which naturally resides within each, and every one of us. **It's the only way to dissolve depression, anxiety and all those happiness-destroying thoughts and feelings which arise within us.**

But let's not get ahead of ourselves because we must first check out how to destroy this second harmful layer of: *Mistakes = Punishment + Going Wrong = Missing Out,* which is currently suffocating the *Masterpiece of YOU* and stopping you from creating your depression-free future.

So how can we tear down this second depression-causing layer as fast as possible?

Well, that's exactly what we're going to be delving into in the next chapter, so I'll see you there!

6

WHY WE DO, WHAT WE DO?

It's a fact, that we LOVE to beat ourselves up when we're simply *down in the dumps*, or in the *pits of hell* and struggling in depression, but why do we do it?

After all, in depression we're usually asking (or at least wishing) everyone would be more kind and gentle towards us, but are WE kind and gentle to ourselves? Hell, no! We're our own worst enemy!

In all honesty, we're asking others to give us, what we won't even give ourselves.

Well, let's turn that around!

Let's follow that famous quote: *Charity begins at home* so we can see, that as soon as we begin to lighten up and start being more compassionate and gentle towards ourselves, the easier it becomes to catapult ourselves up and out of depression.

But first, we must uncover *why* we do it?

Why do we beat ourselves up over our decisions, our choices, our actions, how we look, how we fee, what we think, our past, our future, everything?

The answer lies within this second layer of: *Mistakes = Punishment + Going Wrong = Missing Out.*

You see, if we really look at this formula, which has been planted within our minds since childhood, we can quickly recognise that anytime we feel we're *missing out* in life, we instantly believe it's because WE WENT WRONG SOMEWHERE (or someone else went wrong, *it's their fault*). And what do we do when we start having these thoughts and feelings?

We start beating ourselves up for going wrong, for making the wrong choice, saying the wrong thing, or taking the wrong path. Simply because <u>we cannot imagine there's any other explanation for *why* we're missing out</u>, for why things are going wrong or for why we're not getting what we want.

That's simply because our minds have been wired to believe WE can control an outcome. For example: Our childhood taught us that *if we're good, we'll get and if we're bad, we'll miss out.* We've been led to believe that all results and outcomes are within our hands, within our control. They're simply down to how we perform, behave or act.

It's an extremely damaging belief system which enshrouds much of society, hence, the skyrocketing rates of depression and anxiety.

So, what's the solution?

How can we stop beating ourselves up and begin accepting ourselves wholeheartedly?

After all, if we can't learn to love ourselves, *'warts and all,'* as the saying goes, we'll struggle to free ourselves from the clutches of depression, which is not what we want.

So, let's check out *why* you make the decisions you make and take the actions you take, so you can begin to drop this second harmful layer of: *Mistakes = Punishment + Going Wrong = Missing Out* and step into a depression-free future.

Firstly, imagine you own an extremely precious filing system. It's the only one of its kind in the entire universe. It sits within your mind and this Personal Filing System stores your private collection of beliefs regarding certain situations, people, places, things, events, etc. Let's call it your **Personal Cloud Storage Centre**, as it stores absolutely everything you know, have experienced and believe.

Your Personal Cloud Storage Centre

Now, imagine you've just won a car and you're allowed to select its colour from the choices below, which colour of car would you choose?

- White Car
- Red Car
- Green Car
- Blue Car
- Black Car
- Purple Car

Did one colour <u>instantly stand out</u> from the rest? Was it an easy decision for you, or were you struggling over a couple of colours before you eventually settled on one?

Now, if we take a microscope to this rapid-fire, colour selection process we would see that once you were asked the question: *"Which colour of car would you choose?"* Your mind instantly scanned the entire contents of your **Personal Cloud Storage Centre** and searched for any strong-held beliefs regarding colours. For example, it searches for things like; favourite colours, colours you dislike, other beliefs regarding specific colours; red goes faster or white is hard to keep clean.

Then, after this rapid analysis, your **Personal Cloud Storage Centre** brings a colour to the forefront of your mind. Which is the colour you end up selecting.

Your Personal Cloud Storage Centre Brings The Best Colour To The Forefront Of Your Mind

This specific colour is the one in **greatest alignment** with all the beliefs stored within your Personal Cloud Storage Centre.

Now, even though this is an extremely simple colour selection process, this is the very same process which occurs with all our decisions, even the most complex ones.

This is how all our mind's process information and make choices. Our *Personal Cloud Storage Centre* always generates the best possible answer or choice for us, at any given moment in time, without fail.

But, let's not leave it there because if we ever want to live a depression-free life we must truly understand how our decisions relate directly to this second depression-causing layer of: *Mistakes = Punishment + Going Wrong = Missing Out.*

So, let's take this up a notch and meet John, he's just been given a couple of new job opportunities and is unsure about which one is right for him.

John is faced with the following two choices:

- **Job Opportunity A:** A new position within his current company which comes with many promotional opportunities, due to his length of time with the company.

41

- **Job Opportunity B**: A position with a new company, which comes with no chance of promotion but has a much higher salary.

How does John decide which choice is right for him?

Well, in the exact same way, your mind selected the best colour for the car in the previous example, John's mind collates all the information he has available to him (including gut instincts, intuition, beliefs, knowledge and experiences) and comes up with a decision which best aligns with his most important beliefs, wants, desires, priorities and goals, held within his *Personal Cloud Storage Centre*.

Which in this instance, is Job Opportunity A; the position with his current company.

John's Mind Brings The *Best Choice* To The Forefront Of His Mind

As a result, of his choice everyone at the company is extremely happy John has decided to stay. However, six months down the track, everything rapidly goes downhill. The company goes bust and John gets made redundant.

As you can imagine, John is naturally frustrated and starts kicking himself for not taking the job with the other company (which is still going strong).

Understandably, John is extremely angry and with his mind under a great deal of stress, he starts beating himself up:

- *Why didn't I see it coming?!*
- *I should've known better!*
- *Others told me not to trust the company!*
- *Why didn't I trust my instincts?!*
- *Why didn't they tell me before I took the position?!*
- *If only I'd taken the other job, life would've been okay now!*

As you can imagine his self-defeating thought processes, go on and on, until he's crippled his mindset. So much so, he becomes totally depressed and feels completely defeated.

I'm sure we've all faced similar scenarios to John, at least once in our lifetime.

However, we must be aware that **anytime we link our external circumstances or outcomes, to any so-called wrong decisions or us not being good enough in some way, we're reinforcing and strengthening this second layer of:** *Mistakes = Punishment + Going Wrong = Missing Out.*

Which is not what we want. We want to loosen its grip on us, so we can tear it down completely.

So, let's take another look at John's decision and recognise, that his choice was based upon all the information he had available to him at that time. In other words, he chose the best choice for him at that precise moment in time (if it wasn't the best choice, his mind would have brought a different option forward for him).

We also need to remember that he didn't know then, what he knows now. We must always take this into account with all our own decisions, choices or actions.

We are ALWAYS doing our best and making the best choice for us <u>at the time</u> of our decisions.

In fact, take a moment to recall a decision, choice or action you're currently beating yourself up over. Or a past event, decision or action you're struggling to let go of.

Something you're saying one of the following to:

- *If only…*
- *I should've known better*
- *Why didn't I….*
- *I'm so stupid for…. (or for not….)*
- *I should've……. instead!*

Now when you recall this scenario, how does it feel knowing that **you were doing your best at the time** of your decision?

Truth is, given the very same circumstance, with the exact same files stored within your *Personal Cloud Storage Centre*, you would make the same decision if we time-travelled you back to that <u>exact moment in time</u>.

This is because it was the best choice for you <u>at that time</u>.

It was the decision which best served all your most important priorities, at that moment in time.

So why beat yourself up for not knowing better? Or for making the so-called wrong decision? It was never wrong. It was the right and best decision for you at that time. If it wasn't the best choice, you never would have made it.

Always remember, anytime you beat yourself up over the times you feel you didn't do the best thing in the situation, or things could've or should've been done differently, look again!

Because from where you're sitting today, the situation has ALREADY happened. The decision has ALREADY been made. The outcome has ALREADY occurred and you're completely aware of all the consequences of the decision, and all this *feedback* has simultaneously updated your *Personal Cloud Storage Centre*. You now have new, updated *'files'* in the database of your mind.

You are now looking back at the past with a much greater knowledge base.

After Any Decision You Have The Advantage Of A *Birds Eye View*

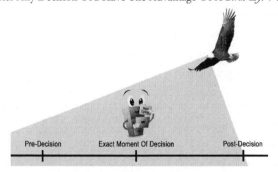

Pre-Decision   Exact Moment Of Decision   Post-Decision

You're now able to see a *bird's eye view* of the complete timeline of your decision.

You can see everything, from where you stand today, right back to the exact moment of the decision. Including, everything that lead up to the event with brand new eyes.

You didn't have this larger perspective when you made the decision you made.

So yes! Today, you may make a different decision given the same situation but remember, your mind now has an updated database, with a much greater variety of information to work from.

After any decision, we are always smarter irrelevant to whether it turned out to be in our favour or not. That's the beauty of *hindsight.*

Although, hindsight also has a much darker side to it, depending upon how we use it.

In fact, how we use hindsight can rapidly determine whether we drive ourselves deeper into the cycle of depression or lift ourselves up and out of it, at a great rate of knots.

How are you currently using the gift of hindsight in your life?

If you're like many people suffering in depression, you're more than likely using hindsight as a *weapon* to beat yourself up with.

Instead, of using it as the helpful tool it was intended to be.

The quickest way to discover if you're wielding hindsight as a mighty weapon against yourself, is to simply ask:

- Do I frequently criticise myself for not knowing better, for going wrong, for being foolish, for making mistakes or failing, when something doesn't turn out as I expected or wanted it to?

Again, this mindset is simply driven by this layer of: *Mistakes = Punishment + Going Wrong = Missing Out.*

However, if we ever want to catapult ourselves out of depression, we must lay hindsight down as a weapon, and pick it back up as the helpful *tool* it was intended to be.

For example, when we feel, we've made a so-called mistake in life by failing to hit the bullseye (achieving our goal), we can use hindsight in two ways:

1. **HINDSIGHT AS A WEAPON:** We can beat ourselves up, abuse ourselves, continuously tell ourselves how stupid we are and how we *'should've known better'.*

2. **HINDSIGHT AS A TOOL:** We accept we missed the bullseye this time, but with the use of hindsight we improve our aim and do better next time. After all, it's only AFTER we've thrown the dart (made the decision, taken the action) and seen where it landed, can we assess whether we need to go a little more to the right or to the left next time.

    <u>With the help of hindsight, we're always being guided and directed to the best possible outcome</u>, if only we choose to observe the lessons and adjust our approach in response.

In fact, the faster we fail and use the knowledge gained via hindsight, the more rapidly we'll achieve our desired outcome. But, we must take the first step to gain the necessary knowledge and experience.

The more rapidly we fail, the faster we discover ways to succeed.

From today, start to <u>embrace your decisions</u>. Have fun with them and know, whichever decision you choose today, you are always doing the best with all the information you have available to you.

Never forget, when you use the beauty of hindsight to improve your aim, instead of beating yourself up, you'll get to where you wish to go far more rapidly!

Each Wrong Aim Brings Us Closer To Getting It Right.

We must also remember, anytime we're angry or frustrated with others for doing (or not doing) something we expected, or preferred they did (or didn't do), they're also working from their own *Personal Cloud Storage Centre* (their minds filing system).

Which means, whatever they're doing (or not doing) they believe is the best option for them, at this moment in time.

We must accept this is how everyone's decision making process works. This will allow us to give others the respect to do what feels right for them (instead of trying to change, coerce or manipulate them into doing what we believe is right for them).

Now, this does not mean we simply *'roll over'* and allow others do what they want with us. Not at all, because if others' behaviour, choices or actions affect us in a detrimental way, then we have every right to place a boundary within our relationship. For example, we may need to say, *'this behaviour is not okay with me,'* or *'this relationship is not going to work if you carry on in this manner.'*

However, we must be aware this is not about making the other person's behaviour wrong, it's simply saying to the other person, *'this behaviour is not in alignment with who I am.'* It's about being true to ourselves.

The more honest we are with ourselves and others about what we want and need in life, the faster we'll free our masterpiece (our true selves) from all those hideous societal layers which keep us hidden and stuck in the depths of depression.

Also, as an added bonus, the more authentic we are, the less bothered we are about fitting in. And the less bothered we are about fitting IN, the more rapidly we'll discover people we naturally fit WITH. Resulting in us, creating more deeply connected, authentic relationships, with ease.

Relationships which build us up, rather than tear us down.

Truth is, life dramatically improves and becomes more enjoyable the moment we start living authentically.

From today:

✓ Stop beating yourself up over past decisions or choices, because you were doing your best with all the information you had available to you at the time!

✓ Use hindsight as a tool to improve your aim.

✓ Recognise the faster you fail, the more rapidly you'll discover how to succeed.

✓ If you're unhappy about where a decision has led you, that's okay. Simply follow these 3 steps:

   1. Recognise there's no point looking backwards because you're not going that way.

   2. You must accept the decision has been made. Period. Whether you like it or not, you thought it was the best option for you at the time.

   3. You can simply make a new decision today and begin moving forward in the direction you want to.

✓ Always remember, what's for you will never go by you.

✓ Let go of the past because every single moment you spend looking towards the past (which is dead energy), you are missing the present moment (which is living, vibrant energy). Remember, you can only affect the present moment, you can never change the past.

I'm aware it's not always easy to let go of our past. Therefore, to help you move past your past I'm including the highly effective technique: **Rapidly Cleanse Your Past**.

I highly recommend you complete it as soon as possible, as this will help to release any of that heaviness which is weighing you down and stopping you from rising upwards into a depression-free future.

Rapidly Cleanse Your Past Technique

This technique will help you move forward and drop all those people, beliefs, and regrets holding you back in life.

The first thing you need to do is set aside some private time, as this is a very personal process.

Grab yourself a pen and several pieces of paper and don't over think any part of this process.

Simply, read the questions below and start writing anything and everything that comes to mind.

Be aware, that whatever comes up, has come up for a reason. So, simply write everything down that comes to mind without any opposition.

Remember, there's nobody around to judge you and these are YOUR innermost thoughts and they have nothing to do with anybody else.

So, with that said, let's get started...

Part One

Write down all the people and situations in your life (past and present), which you feel have caused you to suffer in some way or have held you back from creating the life of your dreams.

Note: It's best to write one person or situation at the top of each piece of paper, this will help us later, as we move through the questions.

Part Two

Complete the following five steps for each person or situation you've written down:

1. Take a piece of paper which has a person or situation written at the top and say to yourself, *"I accept what's done, is done"*.

   Now, I'm acutely aware this can be far easier said than done sometimes, but no amount of re-hashing or re-playing of the past within our minds is ever going to change what's already happened.

   The past is dead. We can no longer affect it and we must accept this. However, we **can** affect our future. So, with the person or situation in your mind, recognise that the result is, what it is. Accept this and move on to step number two when you're ready.

2. Now, even though we may have accepted *'what's happened, has happened'*, this does not mean we push down, reject or de-press any of our natural and very understandable feelings we may have regarding a person or situation. For example, we may feel anger, hurt, shame, hostility, frustration, rage, disgust, sadness, etc.

   We must allow ourselves to experience and accept whatever natural feelings arise within us.

   That <u>does not mean</u> we *act out* these emotions towards others, or use them as a destructive force.

The main point to remember is that it's okay to feel what you're feeling regarding any situation. They are your personal feelings and you have every right to feel them.

So, when you feel ready, declare out loud to yourself: *'I have a right to feel [......name whatever you are feeling....Eg. Anger] but now I'm ready to transform these feelings into more positive and empowering ones to create a beautiful future for myself.*

This step is about accepting and acknowledging your honest feelings. Accepting that it's okay to have them. Accepting that they're natural. In fact, you're perfectly human for having them.

(WARNING: Do not misunderstand my words. We have every right to feel what we feel, but we do not have the right to use our negative energy against another. It's our sole responsibility to learn how to deal with and release any negative emotions in a safe and constructive manner. It's never okay for us to use our negative emotions as an *'excuse'* to do harm to ourselves and/or others. In a later chapter, we delve deeper into how to constructively deal with our emotions).

3. After your powerful declaration and with the person/situation still in your mind, write down the answers to the following questions underneath their name or description.

   ▪ How, or in what way, has your life improved because of this person/situation?

   ▪ How has this person/situation created a new path for you?

   ▪ What lessons have you learnt from having this person/situation enter your life? And more importantly, what have you learnt about yourself?

- What valuable qualities, lessons, strengths, etc.,
  would you NOT have discovered about life
  and/or yourself, if this person/situation had not
  shown up in your life?

4. When you feel, you have transformed your feelings
   regarding the person/situation and you can now see
   and feel the powerful reason/s for this occurring
   within your life, pick up the piece of paper associated
   with the person/situation.

   Now, whilst holding the image of the
   person/situation in your mind, say out loud: *"I'm
   grateful for what you have taught me. I'm aware that due to
   everything involved it couldn't have worked out any other way.
   I accept that we are always doing our best with the resources
   we have available to us. I thank you, I forgive you and I
   release you."*

   Then burn the piece of paper.

5. Complete this process for each person and/or
   situation you have written down.

When you burn each piece of paper, see it as a
symbolic burning of your past.

You are burning all those old, outdated or
uncomfortable memories. See them float away, just like
smoke on the air. Dissolving into nothingness and out
of your life forever. Feel yourself being released from
all the *baggage* of your past.

Talking about baggage!

Can you remember the last time you took some
baggage to the airport or train station to head off on
holiday? Security is tight these days, so everywhere we
go, we're constantly reminded that we're 100%

responsible for our own baggage. Therefore, we tend to keep a firm grip on it, don't we?

Now, in the very same way we drag around our physical baggage with us on holiday, it is us who also drags around our mental and emotional baggage.

Our baggage does NOT hold onto us.
We hold onto it!

Therefore, we can choose to leave our mental or emotional baggage behind, anytime we like (just like we can choose to leave our baggage at the airport). All we need to do is simply release our firm grip on the handle and just…LET IT GO.

There's a reason a great majority of self-help advice says to *'let go.'* It means exactly that! Let go of what's holding you back, just drop it. Let it go. Let the handle of your baggage go!

In fact, why not ask yourself right now:

✓ Are you ready to give yourself permission to let go of the baggage holding you back, so you can finally step forward into a brighter and not to mention, lighter, depression-free future?

Now, I highly recommend you complete this *Rapidly Cleanse Your Past Technique* as soon as possible, so you can finally let go of your past to rapidly enhance your happiness, elevate your soul and start walking into your depression-free future.

Always remember, you are beautiful, you are loved and you are supported. Your depression-free life is firmly within your grasp.

See you in the next chapter!

7

MISSING OUT ON THE LIFE YOU WERE MEANT TO HAVE?

In the previous chapter, you learnt that at the time of any decision, choice or action, you're always doing your best with all the information you have available to you. In other words, you simply did what you thought was right for you at that moment in time. However, this usually brings up the question:

"So, if I didn't go wrong in any way, why am I still missing out? And, why is my life still going wrong?"

This is a perfectly natural question when we've been enshrouded within this second depression-causing layer of: *Mistakes = Punishment + Going Wrong = Missing Out* for any length of time.

In fact, this whole layer causes us to strongly believe that we are indeed missing out on the life we were *meant to have*. A life, we believe is attached to the alternative decision or path we never chose.

At first glance, this makes complete sense. However, we must take a closer look.

So, recall a decision-making moment in your life and ask yourself, *'were you ever going to choose the other decision, cjoice or path in that moment?'*

Now, even though another path may have been available to you, you didn't take it.

Why? Because you <u>firmly believed</u> the option you did choose, was the right one for you at that time.

In other words, at the moment of your decision, you chose the best possible choice for you.

Therefore, if you were always going to make the decision you made, or take the action you took (because that was the best possible option for you at that time), how can you miss out on a life you <u>believe</u> you were meant to have? You cannot miss out on what was never going to be yours in the first place.

You made the decision you made. Period.

Therefore, you were never meant to have the other path (well not right now anyway), or else you would have made THAT decision.

Yes! Within our imaginations it's easy to believe the other path is still *'over there,'* just out of reach, taunting us with all those glorious things we believe we're currently missing out on, but look again!

Moment of Decision
(Select the choice based upon all the information we have available to us)

After Decision
(Our Choice Becomes Our Path. The Path We Were Always Going To Take In That Moment)

We Cannot Miss Out, On What, Was Never Ours In The First Place

<u>At the precise moment</u> of our decision, we were never going to take any other path than the one we chose. Therefore, we cannot miss out on what was never ours in the first place.

REALITY CHECK

There's NO missing out on the life we were meant to have, because we're having the life we ARE meant to be having. The one created from our best decisions which were determined by all the information we had available to us.

Now, it's a fact of life whether we wish to believe it or not, that we are always doing our best at the time of any decision. Always.

If we've made a decision in the past which has landed us in a situation today which we're not happy with, that we're not okay with, that's okay. We simply make *another* decision to alter our direction and keep moving forward. We never give up or stop believing in ourselves, simply because life hasn't delivered what we believed it should, in the time frame we expected it to.

Just because our dreams have not come into fruition today (as we expected or wanted them to), does not mean they won't blossom into life tomorrow.

Never forget these **Three Vital Facts of Life**:

1. **Just because we cannot see the seedling growing beneath the soil, does not mean it's not happening.**

   The same principle applies to our dreams. Just because we cannot see obvious movement in our favour, does not mean it's not happening. Life happens *'behind the scenes.'* Be like a seedling. Have the courage to keep taking positive forward action and believe in yourself, even when you're completely covered in darkness.

58

2. **We cannot work with or create anything positive from simple moans and groans.**

   Neither can we grasp anything substantial from constantly re hashing or re-working the past within our minds. We can only work with what we have in front of us. We must begin from where we are and since, every day is a fresh new beginning, what actions can you take today to start moving closer to the depression-free future you so desire and deserve?

3. **Even though we cannot miss out IN life, we can miss out ON life.**

   Unfortunately, many of us *miss life* completely, simply because we're constantly worrying about the future, reminiscing over the past, or moaning and groaning about what we believe *should be* occurring. All the while, WE ARE MISSING OUT ON THE MOMENT, which is all the life we truly have.

   So, ask yourself, how do you want to spend your moments? In the now, living? Or do you prefer to spend your life constantly reviewing the past, which is dead and buried?

Now, in the next chapter we're going to be delving deeper into our mistakes and rapidly dissolving them. This will help catapult you onto the path up and out of depression, so I'll see you there.

8

ARE WE MISTAKEN ABOUT MISTAKES?

As a child, our mistakes were our greatest learning tools. For example: when learning to walk, if we leaned one way too far, stepped incorrectly, or went to fast, we fell over and each time we fell (failed to walk correctly), we got up and tried again a different way, until we eventually worked out what was once, the mysterious *'art'* of walking.

In all honesty, we've only grown up BECAUSE of our mistakes.

Mistakes are how we learn and how we eventually discover the best way of doing things. Think about it, we wouldn't be walking today if it wasn't for all our so-called *mistakes* and *failures* as a child.

In fact, whether we're aware of it or not, there's an extremely natural instinct within us to want to try new things, venture into new territory, be adventurous and explore. It's what we naturally did as children and those feelings are still inherently within us.

However, as adults our adventurer has all but disappeared. That's because along the road, called the journey of life, we've been wrapped up in this second very crippling layer of: *Mistakes = Punishment + Going Wrong = Missing Out*, which causes us to buy-into the illusion that mistakes are bad and should be avoided at all costs.

This forced our natural adventurer and explorer to go underground. We lost touch with a very natural part of ourselves, our adventurer, our *'give it a go'* spirit. Instead, we became afraid of making mistakes, looking foolish or being punished (all thoughts and feelings driven by this second extremely suffocating layer).

But have you ever asked yourself, what <u>are</u> mistakes? What does it even mean, if I make a *mistake?*

Some may say, I've failed or gone wrong somewhere, but the term mistake simply means, I've *'missed the mark.'* It's a MISS-TAKE. No big deal. We're the director of our own life, so we simply do a RE-TAKE until we get it right. Now, it may not be with the same *'leading actors'* the second or third time around, but that's okay because life has a way of sending us exactly who we need, when we need them.

To step into a depression-free future, we must free ourselves from the derogatory and very negative connotations we have associated with the word mistake and start seeing the word MISS-TAKE for what it is. It's the fall of a baby when learning to walk, it's a child incorrectly pronouncing a new word, or us missing the bullseye the first time around. There's absolutely no scent of failure in any of these scenarios.

Only WE attach failure to outcomes.

Truth is, we are all imperfectly human and we're never going to get it right first time. That's impossible! As the saying goes, *to err is human*. **The sooner we accept the reality of our imperfection, the more perfect we feel within ourselves**.

However, let's not leave it there, because there's one thing being comfortable with our own mistakes and another, reacting confidently and positively when others condemn us for making these miss-takes.

So, just for a moment imagine I remark, *'you've made a mistake!'* With a heavy tone of disapproval.

What am I *really* saying? What's being said *behind my words?*

There's two very important points you must be aware of that I'm not saying directly, which are:

1. **I'm telling you I'm not comfortable with people making mistakes or going wrong around me.**

   Which translates to: *I'm not comfortable making mistakes and the fact you're making them, highlights my insecurity and discomfort around them.* Therefore, if someone condemns you for making a miss-take, recognise they have yet to understand the naturalness of miss-takes and how they help us to grow and mature. You now have a much greater level of awareness and understanding than they do. Which means, you're able to help them discover the truth about themselves, life and the world around them.

2. **I'm telling you that <u>I believe</u> you've gone wrong or done the wrong thing.**

Take special note of the words: I believe. Which means, it's purely 100% my opinion. <u>That does not make it fact</u>. It simply means, this is my personal interpretation of the situation and I'm just one measly opinion in a gigantic ocean of over 7,461,059,467 other opinions.

Never get hung up on the opinions of others (remember the ancient tale of the donkey?), because there are as many opinions in this world as there are people.

From today, start to consciously live by facts rather than opinions. Also, trust in what *feels right for you*, not in what others tell you, is right for you.

Now, even though I've just said we should never get caught up in the opinions of others. That does not mean, we move to the opposite extreme and become like that *'old dog who can't learn new tricks.'*

So, what do I mean by this?

Well, have you ever met someone who refuses to accept their MISS-TAKES?

Maybe you tried to show them a better way of doing something but they flatly refused to hear your suggestions. They may have even got heated or hostile towards you. This is the classic *'old dog, new tricks'* mentality.

I'm sure we've all either experienced this type of personality within our lives. Or, maybe we've even been this type of person, once or twice (I know I have).

So, what's going on?

Why the negative reaction to help and assistance?

In all honesty, this reaction is a very natural by-product of this second layer: *Mistakes = Punishment + Going Wrong = Missing Out.*

This self-esteem crushing layer makes us believe a mistake or wrong doing diminishes our worth and inner value as a person. It makes us feel *less than* the next person. It's not true of course, but this second layer which is suffocating and hiding our true beauty and worth in this world, is driving this behaviour.

How can we stop it?

By simply looking at a young child and observing how they respond to our feedback and advice.

When a child does something and we show them a better way, they instantly learn and rapidly grow and improve from it. A very young child does not care or even conceive of the so-called *'mistakes mentality.'* The child is completely innocent. There's no seriousness. They're just trying to learn everything they can and the more they're shown, the more they come alive.

They're thirsty to learn everything they can.

So, instead of believing our miss-takes impact our self-worth in any way, we must reclaim our child-like innocence and open ourselves up to learning and exploring life once again. Which naturally means, we're going to get it wrong sometimes, but who cares?!

This caring too much about what others think has become a great sickness of humanity, which I like to call: **The Adult Sickness of Seriousness**. It needs to be dropped. We must lighten up, open ourselves up to life again and *accept* that in life we're never going to stop learning.

We must drop the foolish thoughts which make us believe that as we get older, we should just 'know it all,' because we don't. It's impossible. There's always more to learn about ourselves, about others, about life, and the world around us.

Open yourself up once again. Become curious. Accept help and assistance and see how rapidly you launch yourself onto the path of growth, maturity, expansion and abundance.

I'll finish this chapter with two very solid truths about life:

> *The only true wisdom is in knowing you know nothing.*
> ~ Socrates ~

> *If you understand everything, you must be misinformed.*
> ~ Japanese Proverb ~

9

THE THIRD DEPRESSION-CAUSING LAYER

It's time to delve into the third, final and innermost layer, which is currently enshrouding the pristine *Masterpiece of YOU* in darkness.

This is the <u>most harmful layer</u> of all.

It's this very layer which is responsible for **causing us to feel small and insignificant in life**. It also causes us to fear sharing our beautiful and much-needed light, talents, voice, abilities and love, out into the world around us. This layer is known as the layer of: **Measure Up + Prove Your Worth**.

1st Depression-Causing Layer:

Good = Getting + Right = Rewards

2nd Depression-Causing Layer:

Mistakes = Punishment + Going Wrong = Missing Out

3rd Depression-Causing Layer:

Measure Up + Prove Your Worth

<u>This is the core</u>. This is the innermost, foundational layer into which the other two previous layers are so gracefully weaved into. Therefore, if we can tear down this layer and we do it the right way, the other two layers will fall like a house of cards and your pristine masterpiece will be set free, so you can finally begin to flourish once again.

This detrimental layer of: **Measure Up + Prove Your Worth** leads us to believe we're not good enough unless we prove otherwise. This crippling layer drives us to continuously strive, no matter the cost, to measure up and PROVE we're good enough, in every area of our life.

This is the most harmful and dangerous layer of all, as it leads us to find our value, our worthiness, within the eyes of others.

If we're entrapped within this layer of: *Measure Up + Prove Your Worth*, we don't accept ourselves and we constantly look to others to *'ASK'* if we're acceptable.

Consequently, we place all our self-esteem, self-respect, self-worth and happiness into the hands of others. **This is a recipe for disaster, since anything that can be given to us, can just as easily be taken away**.

Who wants to live life with their self-esteem and self-worth in the hands of others? It's as if we must *beg* for our worth to be handed back to us. No thank you! That's no way for anyone to live!

So, to tear this tremendously crippling layer down, we must rapidly shift our focus from, allowing others and the outside world to *dictate* our worth and value, to looking within, discovering it and solidifying it within ourselves.

We must discover how to uncover and OWN our beautiful masterpiece within and embrace the magnificent, unbreakable Core Value that comes along with it.

But how do we know if this detrimental layer of: **Measure Up + Prove Your Worth** is currently affecting our life?

Ask yourself:

- Do you feel you're not good enough unless you prove otherwise?
- Do you constantly compare yourself to others to see if you're measuring up?
- If you see others as better off than you, does that make you feel less inside, inferior, or as if you've underachieved?
- If you see yourself as better off than others, does that make you feel superior or above others in any way?
- In relationships, do you feel you should mould yourself into what others want to receive love? Or do you feel you should never *'rock the boat'*, as this may cause others to leave you?
- Do you feel you must *'keep up with the joneses,'* as the saying goes? In other words, do you feel you need the latest gadgets, the best body, the bigger house, the faster car, the most attractive partner or the next best thing, to feel you're a *'somebody'* or you've *'made it'* in life?
- Are you highly competitive or driven by a need to outdo others?
- Do you demand that others constantly prove themselves to you? Whether that's their love, their

loyalty, or their friendship. Or, are you on the other end of this?

- Do you feel you must constantly prove yourself to others? Prove your love, your loyalty, or your friendship?
- If you fail at something, do you personalise the outcome and begin to see yourself as a failure?
- Do you struggle with depression, anxiety or suicidal thoughts?
- If you lose your job, a relationship, or your finances drop below a certain point, do you feel small, worthless or less inside?
- Do you feel you must become a *'somebody'* (a name, a star, the best in your field) otherwise, you're just a nobody?

These are just a few of the common scenarios or mindsets related to this harmful and very toxic layer of: **Measure Up + Prove Your Worth**.

In the next chapter, we're going to start peeling back this toxic layer to reveal the true beauty of YOU. Helping you discover where your TRUE value lies in this world. This will result in you rapidly tearing down this overly suffocating, life-sucking, happiness-destroying layer of: *Measure Up + Prove Your Worth,* so you can finally set the exquisite *Masterpiece of YOU* free to flourish.

See you there!

10

FEEL YOU'RE NOT GOOD ENOUGH?

The only way to truly rip down this totally hideous third layer of: **Measure Up + Prove Your Worth**, is to free ourselves from the illusion that it breeds within us. The illusion that permeates and sabotages every area of our lives; the illusion that we're not good enough just as we are.

First, can you do me a favour? It'll only take a moment.

Please place your hands out in front of you, palms facing upward.

Now look at your hands closely, see all the various grooves which are carved into the palms of your hands. Slowly move upwards and see all the lines where your finger joints are. Keep moving upwards, until your eyes rest upon your fingertips. Take a moment to observe each, and every one of your fingertips.

Can you see there's a unique fingerprint on each, and every finger? No two are alike, every single fingerprint is one-of-a-kind.

It's pretty awesome when you think about it, because in a world of over 7,461,059,467 people, every single fingerprint, on every single finger, is totally unique. And just like, every single fingerprint across this entire globe is **authentically unique**, so are you.

You are a one-of-a-kind rarity.

You are a priceless and very beautiful masterpiece, amongst a crowd of over 7,461,059,467 people.

Think about that for a moment.

<u>There's just one YOU</u> in this entire world of over 7,461,059,467 other unique people.

How can you ever doubt your value, when nobody across this entire globe can replace you?

That's how unique you are! You're irreplaceable.

Don't believe me? No worries!

Simply, take a moment, look around and see for yourself.

Can you find anyone, who is just like you?

Even if you have an identical sibling, you are not that alike, because <u>nobody</u> across this entire globe has:

- The *exact* same past as you.
- The *exact* same life experiences as you.
- The *exact* same beliefs or *'pool of knowledge'* as you.
- The *exact* same skills, talents, likes or dislikes as you.
- And the list goes on and on… Regarding all the ways you are different from others.

There's NOBODY, other than you who's just <u>like you</u>, in this entire world and <u>that is</u> your beauty! <u>That is</u> your power! <u>That is</u> your strength! <u>That is</u> your immense Core Value.

The reality is, you are so very important and valuable to this world because…

There's never been another you, nor will there ever be again. No one has ever walked your path before, nor will they ever again.

You are quite literally, the one-of-a-kind exquisite *Masterpiece of YOU* and this world needs you to see it. It needs you to OWN your magnificence, because **it's YOU and everything you are, that's needed in this world today**; your energies, your talents, your experiences, your thoughts and feelings, your strengths, and yes! Even your weaknesses too, everything that you have wrapped up inside of that beautiful *Masterpiece of YOU* is needed.

Remember, it's a proven fact that NOTHING is put here that's useless and absolutely NOTHING is a *spare part* in the grand circle of life.

In other words, **if you are here; you are needed.** And, without you, this world would be missing something of tremendous valuable.

Now, the danger with this layer of: *Measure Up + Prove Your Worth* is that you may *feel* there's some truth in what I'm saying, you may even *want* to believe that you are immensely important and contribute so much value to this world. However, there may still be a tiny little voice in the back of your mind saying, *'that can't be right! I can't have value for no reason at all! I must DO something! I have to become a somebody!'*

If you are thinking anything like that, it's okay. It's a perfectly natural response. After all, we've had a lifetime's conditioning; from our parents, our schooling, our work places, our relationships, our religious institutions, instilling in us that we are not enough, *just as we are.'* We had to prove we're worthy, prove we're deserving, prove we had significance, prove we could conform, fit in, be good, or do the right thing.

We've been wrapped up within this layer of: *Measure Up + Prove Your Worth* (along with the other two) from such an early age, that it's become second nature for us to feel we must EARN our place in this world. We must measure up or be left behind.

It's never been enough for us to just simply be ourselves.

However, we must drop this conditioning if we ever want to step into a depression-free future.

How do we do that?

Well, have you ever truly taken in the immense beauty of the night sky? In fact, why not go out tonight and lay under the stars and observe the magnificent landscape called the *'night sky.'*

If you wait long enough, the night sky will share **four truths about life** with you, which are:

1. **Every single star shines in its own unique way.**
   Some stars shine bright and others, not-so bright. However, they all shine and it's all these differences of light within the stars which create something of immense beauty; the night sky. It has a magnificent beauty.

2. **The stars are just being themselves.**
   They're not performing or going out of their way to *'outdo'* the next star. They're just being natural and shining THEIR rare light, in a way that only they can. That's what makes the night sky so remarkable.

3. **You are just like one of those magnificent stars.**
   You have a rare kind of light that only you can shine into this world. It's the radiant light that shines when you're just being

yourself. That's what makes you so rare and beautiful, you are a one-of-a-kind light in this world.

4. **Yes, you are different from others**.

That's what makes you such an essential part in creating the amazing and beautiful landscape of life. Recognise, <u>the beauty of the night sky is only possible BECAUSE each star shines differently</u> from any other. It's the different qualities of each star that CREATES the beauty.

Be sure to recall, these four truths next time you feel *'unworthy'* or *'not good enough'* because you are not like others.

Your value in this world is <u>not</u> found in being like others, it's found in simply being YOU.

From today, begin dropping this layer which makes you feel you must *Measure Up + Prove Your Worth,* because it's all an illusion.

You don't have to *'prove your worth'* to anyone.

Start feeling proud of who you are because the truth is, it doesn't matter if you don't act, dress or fit in with others expectations or ideals of you, you were never meant to!

You were meant to be an original, one-of-a-kind masterpiece, that's why you were created as one.

AN ULTIMATE FACT OF LIFE: *Since you are so very special and unique to this world, by default, you can never be in any way 'less than' anybody else. It's impossible. You are an original, just like everyone else.*

Next time you compare yourself to others, remember, that if two things are to be compared and one judged as more superior than the other, they must be <u>exactly alike</u>.

In other words, there's no point comparing apples and oranges, or kangaroos and rabbits.

So, how can YOU be placed beside anyone else and compared?

There isn't anyone to compare you to.

You are simply you; a rare and extremely valuable person who <u>contributes in ways, only you can</u>.

Any comparison is impossible. Not to mention, it's a complete waste of your time, energy and talents.

Now, ask yourself:

• Does anyone have the same perspective of this world as you? Can anyone else see life through your eyes?

You see, your perspective is something that's sacred to you and you alone.

I also have my own unique perspective (just like everyone else) and that's how we all bring value to each other's lives. By sharing our unique views of the world around us. Our unique life paths. There's nothing more valuable than that. It's how we all grow and learn from each other.

Without your unique perspective, this world would be missing out on something massively valuable. There would be a specific energy missing from this globe. So please, don't be selfish and keep your unique perspective, talents, voice, beauty and skills to yourself.

This world needs who you are!

We all need you to unveil the beautiful one-of-a-kind masterpiece that lies hidden within you.

As of today, stand up and own your uniqueness. Feel it in your cells and deep inside your heart that you're so very special, because it's an absolute fact of life that <u>you</u> <u>matter</u>.

From this day forward don't let anyone, including yourself, tell you that who you are is not good enough or not right. *Only you can bring the essential qualities 'of you' to this system we call the universe.*

You are one-of-a-kind for that very reason!

This world needs YOU. It does not need carbon copies. That's why your contribution is so very important because only you can:

✓ Love like you do.

✓ Think like you do.

✓ Move like you do.

✓ Communicate like you do.

You are always positively contributing to others' lives in a way that only you can.

And, do you want to know the best part?

It's not even something you have to *try and do*, just be yourself.

Trust that whatever situation you are placed in, you are meant to be there for a reason. You are meant to learn from others, and others are meant to learn from you.

That's why it's so very important for you to be here. There are ways you can help others, motivate others and enhance the lives of others, in ways that only you can.

Absolutely no one can take your place!

Why do you think no one has the same finger print as you?

Because that's **your authentication mark**. That's the mark that *proves* you are the one and only original *Masterpiece of YOU* and nobody, can take your place.

From today, start accepting yourself, respecting yourself, respecting your own inner voice, uncover your beautiful masterpiece and **believe in who you are. The universe does, that's why you're here!**

11

YOU ARE THE PRIZE!

Are you beginning to see your immense value in this world, isn't dependent upon or derived from any external achievements, awards, accolades, marital status, attractiveness, job title, passes or fails, boob size or bank balance?

Your Core Value Is You.

'*You*' are the highly-valuable piece of puzzle you've been searching for.

You are the prize!

This is a fact, whether you choose to believe it or not, but why would you want to leave your tremendous value on the table and simply walk away from it? Why would you turn your back on yourself and everything you are?

Be aware, the tremendous value IS YOU. It's all yours. So why not claim it?

Only you can bring to this world, everything that you have to offer. Therefore, your massive Core Value is an integral part of you. IT IS YOU.

Which means, it doesn't matter how many times you may fall over (just like a baby learning to walk), or how many miss-takes you make, you still have your magnificent Core Value.

YOUR CORE VALUE CAN NEVER BE COMPROMISED

If your Core Value comes from your unique personality and life path, how can it *ever* be compromised? Anything you do simply *adds* to the uniqueness of you and your beauty, which continues to reinforce and build your tremendous value.

NEVER FORGET:

✓ No comparison between yourself and others is ever possible.

✓ Nobody can make your specific contribution to this world.

✓ Your life and life path is totally unique to you, and you alone. <u>You are even completely unique across all centuries of existence</u> because nobody has ever walked your path before and nor will they ever again. That's 100% unique alright!

Who you are, matters.

12

THE TRUE JOURNEY OF LIFE

If we ever believe our life has *gone wrong* somehow, then we need to be aware this simply means we have yet to truly understand the natural process or journey of life.

We also need to be aware that if we ever want to release ourselves from the clutches of depression, understanding the true journey of life is a must.

First, take a moment to look at the image below.

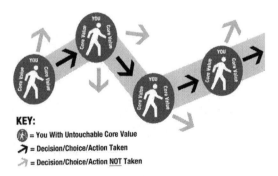

KEY:
= You With Untouchable Core Value
= Decision/Choice/Action Taken
= Decision/Choice/Action NOT Taken

Now, as you look at the image, you'll begin to see that every decision we make *creates* our journey called *'life.'*

Today we choose option B, which now becomes <u>our new path</u>. We walk for a while. Another decision or choice comes along, now based on our beliefs at the time, we choose option B again. Now, that becomes <u>our new life path</u>. Then A, then B, then C, and so on...

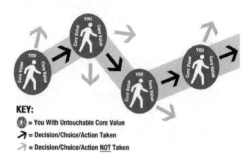

KEY:
= You With Untouchable Core Value
= Decision/Choice/Action Taken
= Decision/Choice/Action <u>NOT</u> Taken

Our life path is ever changing. It's a fluid dance from left to right, it's not ever going to be a straight line because life is an unfolding and continuous process of learning and discovery.

Always remember, at any given time, every single one of us only knows what we know.

This means, we make a decision based upon all the information we have <u>in that moment</u>. Therefore, after gathering all the information we have at our fingertips, a decision is made. Take careful note of those words.

'A' Decision Is Made

- NOT a right decision
- NOT a wrong decision
- ✓ Just simply... 'A' decision

In life, there's never a wrong decision, choice or direction. There's also never a right decision, choice or direction in life either. There are simply *decisions* we make at any given moment in time, using all the information that's available to us. It's these very decisions which create and carve out our unique journey called *'life.'*

If we don't like any outcomes of our decisions, no worries! We have now learnt we may need to do it differently next time, so we adjust our decisions accordingly.

Begin to see your life as a *collection* of life experiences, lessons and learnings.

Life has never been about pass or fail, or right versus wrong. Nor has it ever been about worthy versus unworthy, that's just BS societal conditioning.

Life is a grand journey of continuous growth and learning. Where one event leads to another, which leads on to another and on to another and so on.

The words to remember are; LIFE IS GROWING YOU. It's preparing you for what's to come. What we learn from one chapter of our life, helps us in the next chapter. That's just how life works, it's a process. It's an unfolding of wisdom, it's not a race.

So, in the tough times, believe in yourself and know that you have the strength, the abilities, the courage and more than enough character, to get through whatever it is you're faced with. Life simply gives you trials, so you can uncover these wonderful qualities within yourself.

How else would you discover what you're truly capable of?

Also, be aware that no matter what you're facing in life, your Core Value lies inside you 100% of the time. IT IS YOU and everything you are.

Therefore, there's never a moment your immense value in world, is in danger.

Never forget, this world needs a first-class version of YOU, not a second-rate imitation of another.

There are NO carbon copies in this world, so please *'own'* that prime piece of real estate you are standing on, because wherever your feet move throughout this world, the beautiful and essential qualities of you move too!

SECTION 2

HOW TO FREE YOUR BODY FROM DEPRESSION

13

HOW YOU FEEL, MATTERS!

As we've already discussed, the word depression comes from the Latin word *dēprimere* which means to press down, lower (de-press), or to repress.

However, to get out of depression completely and create a depression-free future, we mustn't leave our understanding at the level of our mind. We must also observe how we de-press or push down our honest feelings and emotions. So, that's exactly what we're going to be covering throughout this section.

So, let's get started.

Now, do you remember hearing any of the following statements as a child?

- *Be quiet. You're too noisy!*
- *What are you up to? You're too quiet!*
- *Would you just sit still for 5 minutes!*
- *Would you just go outside and play!*

As a child, we were constantly bombarded with *'don't do this'* or *'don't do that'* type phrases, but what in the world has this got to do with depression?

Well, if we take a closer look, we'll see that as a child:

- When we played excitedly, we were told we were too noisy and needed to settle down.

- On the other hand, if we were silent or sat still for too long, we were asked what was wrong with us.

Naturally, it didn't take us very long to get confused and start believing that whatever we naturally felt like doing, was wrong in some way.

We learnt very quickly that if we wanted to stop being questioned about our natural behaviour, we had to start conforming or fitting in to our surroundings. Therefore, we learnt to push down (de-press) our natural feelings, our natural spontaneity, to make sure we did the *right thing* in the eyes of others.

From a very young age, we've been conditioned to push aside our bodily responses, our body's wisdom, for acceptance or approval of others.

Instead of feeling what was right for us, we de-pressed our feelings and started listening to what others wanted, what they saw as the right thing for us to do.

The problem with that approach to life, is that what others want, is as varied as the population of this world.

Ask yourself, have you ever done something you KNEW felt wrong, but you went ahead and did it anyway, only to regret it later?

I'm sure we all have. Again, this is the same childhood conditioning of *overriding* our own feelings to follow our mind (or others).

**Be aware that our mind belongs to society,
our body does not.**

Our mind can be convinced of anything. However, our body cannot be convinced of anything it doesn't *feel* is the truth.

During depression, have you ever heard things like:

- *Don't make such a big deal about it.*

- *There's no reason for you to feel how you are feeling.*

- *Get over it!*

- *You just need to be more positive.*

- *What have you got to moan about? Your life has everything! How can YOU be depressed?*

These are just a few of the statements or more appropriately called, *judgements* from others, that we must endure during depression.

Naturally, this makes depression even more challenging for us to deal with. Truth is, whether we place the judgement on whether we *should* or *shouldn't* feel a certain way, or others place the judgement, **it does not matter**.

No judgements (opinions) matter, because WE DO FEEL THAT WAY.

It's not about what's seen as right or wrong, it's about what is actually happening.

Life is not about making sure we *act* the so-called right way to fulfil others expectations of us. That's what got us into the *hell-hole* of depression in the first place!

Life is about being true to ourselves.

Remember, to get out of a state of de-pression, we need to start expressing who we truly are and moving in alignment with what feels right for us.

We need to drop all the layers thrown onto us by society, because every single one of us, doesn't fit into any perfectly crafted box given to us by society.

Any labels like mental illness or mental disorder are simply *handed-out,* when we don't *fit the mould* of what others want us to be.

Ask yourself, is fitting into or being well-adjusted to a sick and chaotic society a measure of health, intelligence or sanity?

I think not and that's all the *usual* treatments for depression are attempting to do. Make you *fit into* today's society. Or at the very least, into one of its manufactured boxes.

However, if we want to create a depression-free future for ourselves, we must stop denying or *pushing down* our honest feelings because that's when *de-pression* begins and continues to grow within us.

Here's the ultimate truth:

The longer we deny and de-press our honest feelings, the longer we will stay in de-pression. GUARANTEED.

Therefore, to escape the clutches of depression, to lift ourselves out from under and rise upwards into a depression-free future, we must learn to start honouring our own feelings and listen to the deep wisdom of our body.

What do I mean by listening to our body?

Well, if your body **feels** like resting or sleeping (and let's be honest, whose doesn't in the depths of depression?), you need to listen to your body and DO IT.

However, there's one extra catch...

You must rest or sleep, <u>fully</u>.

Now, to understand the term *fully* in the correct context, we must look at what usually happens in our daily lives.

Have you ever noticed that during any activity, your mind kicks in and starts saying, *'what about [......] that needs to be finished? You should be doing that.'* For example: *'Oh, I'm so lazy, I shouldn't be sitting around resting whilst I've got [work] to do.'*

FACT:

When we start having a battle between what we *think* we should be doing versus what we *feel* like doing, we're <u>not</u> doing anything *fully*.

We are neither completing the activity we are attempting to do, nor are we, completing the activity we believe we *should* be doing.

In other words, we achieve nothing but create inner turmoil and make ourselves feel bad (again!).

So, to combat this we must begin to consciously complete all activities FULLY.

We need to get past all those annoying thoughts. The thoughts that continue to say, we *should* be doing this, or *should* be doing that. That's the only way we'll be able to relax and get the rest we require to lift ourselves up and out of depression.

(NOTE: In the next chapter, you'll discover the scientific proof which reveals how rest and relaxation, along with listening to your body, can rapidly lift you out of depression).

From today, commit to listening to your body for at least 21 DAYS and see how your depression starts to lift. Trust me, you'll be surprised how good you begin to feel.

In fact, there's a scientific reason for this *'feel good'* feeling, which I'll elaborate on in the next chapter but for now, here's some tips to improve this whole process for you.

Whilst learning to listen to your body, be sure to follow these five steps:

1. When all those naggy, judgmental thoughts arise (and they will), hear those thoughts as the voice of someone you completely dislike or find annoying. Trust me, you won't listen to them anymore.

2. Recognise these judgements as mere opinions. It's an *opinion* that you're lazy when you need a rest, it's NOT A FACT.

3. Start living by facts, rather than opinions. For example, if your body wants to sleep, that's a fact. If you *think* you're lazy because you need that sleep, that's an opinion. **The key is to start listening to your body, not your mind**.

4. If your body wants to sleep all day, then sleep, and when your mind attacks you with all those judgmental statements (and it will). Say to yourself, *'that's okay, call me lazy, call me a failure, they're just opinions. The FACT is my body wants sleep and my body knows best.'*

5. Don't be hard on yourself, slowly work your way into this. To complete activities (or non-activities) FULLY takes conscious effort. It took me around

three days to get into the swing of this. I mean, before I could fully relax, guilt-free and feel *allowed* to put aside all those usual judgements. I had to make a firm decision and commit to listening to my body but I assure you, the rewards were worth it. So, don't delay! Try it for yourself, starting today!

There are even philosophies from both the East and West which acknowledge the vital importance of listening to our body and completing activities *fully*.

From the West, the renowned psychologist William James (1842 – 1910) stated:

"Nothing is so fatiguing as the eternal hanging on of an uncompleted task."

From the East, is a more potent observation from the mystic Osho (1931 – 1990) who observed:

"There is ONE fundamental thing about life: Any experience that has not been fully lived will hang around you, will persist saying 'finish me' - 'live me' - 'complete me.' Every experience wants to be completed, wants to be finished. Once completed it evaporates; but incomplete it tortures you, it haunts you, it attracts your attention."

From today, start listening to your body. Start trusting yourself again because the rewards are worth it!

(**Important Note:** If you have severe depression where you *'feel'* like harming yourself and/or another, do I mean that you should follow these feelings? Absolutely not! Do not harm yourself or others. Under NO circumstance is that condoned. Also, be aware, those *'feelings'* are actually <u>thoughts</u> driven from our mind. However, they still need to be released in a safe and constructive manner. Therefore, if you do feel like hurting another and/or yourself, please jump ahead to the *'Experiencing Great Anger'* chapter of this book and be sure to seek professional advice in your local area).

Now let's look at the other side of the coin for a moment.

What happens if you cannot sleep?

Well, that's okay too! Don't fight it and cause unnecessary tension or frustration inside.

Remember, the more we fight against ourselves, the more de-pression we cause and we don't want any more.

So, if you cannot sleep, simply complete one of the techniques included within the Resources Section of this book.

✓ Start using the time *positively*, instead of condemning yourself and/or your body.

✓ Start working with whatever situation arises, instead of *wishing* it was different.

✓ The only way to transform a situation, is to *work with* the *'ingredients'* we've been given.

From today, start listening to your body. Start being gentle with yourself again because that's how your body will look after you. If you just, allow it.

I want to rest, but I can't!

Now, I'm sure a handful of people reading this book, may be screaming at me right now saying, *'I want to rest but I can't! I've got work to do, others to look after, duties to fulfil.'*

Yes, you may be right. We all have many tasks we need to complete daily.

The question I have for you is this: *Is work more important than your health and state of mind?*

Of course, your health is the priority. So, if you have nothing to lose EXCEPT your depression, why not commit to putting your own health first for the next 21 days? You'll be glad you did.

Additionally, if we do have others to look after, especially children, we have a GREATER responsibility to look after ourselves.

In fact, if you knew your children were in the same position you are in right now, what advice would you give them?

I'm sure it would be to look after their own health first, because it's a priority.

It's not selfish to put our own health first, it's vital!

14

GROUNDBREAKING SCIENCE SHOUTS 'STOP!' – WILL YOU LISTEN?

Science reveals that our senses gather some 11 million bits of information from our en vironment, every second, of every day. Now as if, that wasn't enough to handle, studies also show we're now being constantly bombarded by an average of 5,000 advertising messages per day!

Is there any wonder we're all overwhelmed, stressed or mentally exhausted?

We're constantly being swamped with so much stimuli, that our minds are struggling to find five minutes to *'switch off'* in this new, fast-paced world.

But, that's not the worse part!

You see, scientists recently discovered that when our minds become tired or overwhelmed, we can register life experiences, however we're not able to process or *'digest them'* effectively. In other words, we struggle to make sense of the world around us and our thoughts, feelings and experiences remain *'unresolved'* within our minds.

As a result, all these *'unresolved'* issues, pile up and create a *'backlog'* within our minds.

This backlog not only causes mental exhaustion and overwhelm but it also diminishes our ability to deal with the world around us. Our minds are swamped and have no *'free space'* to consume or process any additional information.

Is your mind currently in a state of overload?

Are you experiencing any of the following?

- Feel like hiding under the duvet all day?
- Wish you could just escape from the world?
- Feel overwhelmed or mentally exhausted?
- Easily confused?
- Feel on edge or emotionally vulnerable?
- Regularly on the brink of tears or anger, but you don't know why?
- Suffering from depression?
- Make silly errors of judgment?
- Forgetful?
- Unable to complete simple everyday tasks?

If you nodded *'yes'* to any of the above experiences, you can be sure your brain is overwhelmed and requires de-cluttering asap!

So, what's the solution?

Well, fortunately the solution is simple.

However, before I reveal the scientifically proven 20-minute solution to declutter your mind and free yourself from mental overwhelm, we must first delve deeper into *"why"* we experience overwhelm in the first place.

After all, it's one thing fixing a problem and another, preventing it from happening ever again.

The great news is, we're going to resolve both in this chapter.

So, let's get started.

Over 50 years ago scientists discovered a hidden rhythm inside each and every one of us, which consists of a period of increased or *'active'* energy for around 1.5-2 hours, then it dives into a period of fatigue for around 20 minutes or so.

So, if we imagine our energy curving upwards for a couple of hours; this is when we have elevated physical and mental alertness and energy. We're running on all cylinders and we're at our peak performance levels.

Then, our energy dives into a valley or trough for around 20 minutes or so. This is when our body-mind system is replenishing any depleted resources, our mental processes are *'catching up'* on any unresolved messages (in other words, we're *'making sense'* of the previous two hours) and our entire system is refueling itself in preparation for the next activity phase.

Which again, sees our energy curve rise upwards for the next couple of hours, before it dives back into a vital rest and replenishment phase for around 20 minutes or so.

This constant undulation of rising and declining energy levels continues throughout our waking and sleeping hours.

Scientists called this undulating rhythm the **B**asic **R**est - **A**ctivity **C**ycle (or BRAC for short).

Basic Rest *(20 Minutes)* - Activity/Energy *(1.5 - 2 Hours)* Cycle

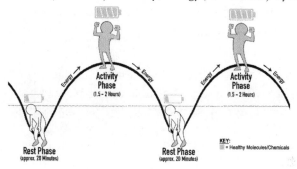

Scientists also discovered that once a cell within our body-mind system commits to division, it also follows this very same BRAC timetable.

Our system requires around 20 minutes to build up an optimal concentration of Cyclin (a messenger molecule that facilitates the process of cell division) before the actual cell division starts to take place, which takes approximately 1.5 - 2 hours to complete.

Cell Division Adheres To The Basic Rest Activity Cycle (BRAC)

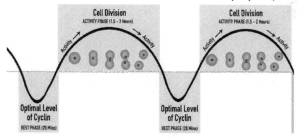

This scientific discovery is huge. As it illustrates the fact that **our ENTIRE SYSTEM and fundamental processes within our body-mind system rely on the Basic Rest - Activity Cycle**, and if this is functioning correctly, all our vital cells can complete their natural

processes with ease. Keeping us in a healthy and strong state (mentally, emotionally and physically).

In fact, here's a glimpse as some of the health-giving, vital processes the BRAC affects:

✓ **Autonomic Nervous System:** The *control system* for your whole system. It controls organ function, heart rate, digestion, respiration, perspiration rate, sexual arousal, among many other vital operations.

✓ **Endocrine System:** Influences almost every cell, organ and function within your body. It's *fundamental* in regulating mood, growth and development, tissue function, cell growth, metabolism, sexual function and reproductive processes.

✓ **Immune System:** Made up of a network of cells, tissues and organs which work together to protect your body.

✓ **Lymphatic System:** A vital part of your circulatory and immune system.

✓ **Circulatory System:** A vast network of organs and vessels responsible for the flow of blood, nutrients, hormones, oxygen and other gases to and from cells. When the circulatory system is not functioning correctly we struggle to fight disease or maintain a healthy internal environment.

It's clear to see, this Basic Rest - Activity Cycle (BRAC) is more powerful than its simplistic name suggests. As it controls every aspect of our lives; from our cell growth to our sexual arousal, from our energy levels to our emotional well-being, from our organ function to our digestion, it even impacts how long we stay in a depressive state (mentally, emotionally and physically).

As the scientists delved deeper, into this *little-known* rhythm they found that the 20-minute Rest Phase of the BRAC is our bodies *'scheduled maintenance program'*.

It's an essential process which allows our entire body-mind system the time to not only replenish our internal resources *(for example; vital, health-giving chemicals, hormones, nutrients, etc.)* which have been depleted in the previous 1.5 - 2-hour Activity Phase, but it also gives our system the time it requires to complete the vital *'behind the scenes'* processes which keep us in tip-top condition, such as; cell division and tissue regeneration. All of which keep us firing on all cylinders.

Which means, our entire body-mind system is refueled and powered-up to be in peak condition (mentally, emotionally and physically) for the next Activity Phase of around 2 hours. **Therefore, if we help our system out; it helps us out!**

If we plan our days, as best we can, around 2 hours of activity versus 20 minutes of rest, we'll be working in alignment with this fundamental Basic Rest – Activity Cycle which is the foundation of our entire body-mind system.

Basic Rest *(20 Minutes)* - Activity/Energy *(1.5 - 2 Hours)* Cycle

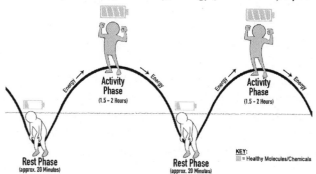

Now, it's not always possible to take a vital Rest Phase at the end of every Activity Phase, since emergencies can crop up, every now and then.

Fortunately, for us, the BRAC comes with some in-built flexibility to cater for our ever-changing environments.

This harks back to our caveman days, when our ancestors were being chased by saber-toothed tigers and the like.

As humans, we needed to be able to respond to serious life and death dangers within our environments. It was a matter of survival, so we couldn't simply sit back and *'wait'* for our systems to replenish themselves, when a saber-toothed tiger was chomping at our heels!

Therefore, in times when our internal resources are depleted yet, we still need to exert additional mental or physical effort to survive, our system *'fuels up'* our internal resources, so we can rapidly respond to the danger.

It does this by flooding our entire system with stress hormones to *'power us'* through the short-term emergency.

Our System Is *Topped Up* With Stress Hormones
To Face The Danger!

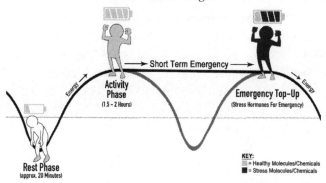

Simply put, our system *loans us some additional resources* to get us through our challenges. **However, just like any loan we must pay it back, with interest!**

For example; if we've missed a vital Replenishment break during the Rest Phase of the BRAC (because we were facing a short-term emergency), instead of requiring the usual 20 minutes to recharge and replenish our system, we may now require 40 minutes to fully replenish our *internal bank* of resources; lifting our system *out of debt*, normalizing our levels, and returning us to an optimal state of overall health and well-being.

Our System Instantly Replenishes Our Internal Resources
After Extended '*Rest Phase*'

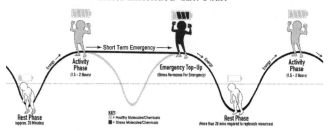

However, we don't live in a world of short-term emergencies anymore, do we?

Something is always demanding our attention! Everything seems of high importance and must be dealt with now. As a result, we're all struggling to find time for ourselves and for the much-needed rest breaks our entire system requires to function correctly.

So, unlike our ancestors who had REAL, *life and death* emergencies to face and could easily find the time in their slow-paced world to chill-out, relax and tell tales about it over the campfire for years to come. We don't have that luxury!

We must *find time* to hold down one or more jobs, build a career, continue with ongoing education (to keep the said job or career), create a family, pay the rent/mortgage, find quality time for the family we've just created and don't forget, we need to look after that same family by making the money from the job that we're trying to hold onto, by hitting all those job quotas and targets. Which means, we may need to stay late or work long hours to feed the family that's crying out for our time and attention! We also need to keep our home clean and tidy, just like our body of course, because we've got to exercise regularly, go to the gym, stay in shape, be fit, look attractive, eat healthy, and how could we forget?! We need to tweet about it, email it, text it, Facebook it, pin it, not to mention, find time to answer other people's tweets, Facebook and email messages because we'd hate them to think we're ignoring them, right? And what about birthdays? We must not forget anybody's birthday. Then there's social gatherings, creating the perfect romantic relationship, visiting family and friends, improving ourselves, and last, but not least, we have that famous motivational advice which tells us to *'take more control of our life!'*

Is there any wonder we are all so stressed?!

We're all struggling to find time for any rest and relaxation, nowadays. However, the **stone-cold truth** is, if we constantly refuse to find time in our busy schedules for a much-needed *Replenishment Break*, we start shifting into what I call; *The Emergency Stress Mode*.

<u>The Emergency Stress Mode</u>

This is when our body-mind system believes we're constantly facing emergencies; one after the other. As if, we can never break free from the saber-toothed tiger chomping at our heels. In response, it <u>constantly dumps</u> *Emergency Stress Hormones* into our system, to super-charge our internal resources to face the dangers.

After all, our system believes the only reason we'd miss an essential Rest + Replenishment Break is if, we're facing a life and death emergency.

By not including vital Rest + Replenishment Breaks throughout our days, we're constantly flooding our system with stress hormones, which causes us to remain in this *Emergency Stress Mode, 24/7*, which simultaneously depletes our natural supply of healthy chemicals, molecules and hormones within our system.

Emergency Stress Mode: Results In A Depressed System

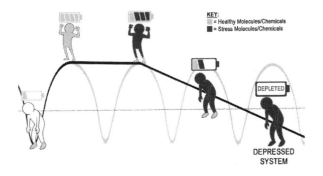

Our systems were not built to run this way. We were never meant to use these short-term emergency *'boosters'* as a lifestyle choice or on a permanent basis. They were intended to be used in the very same way, we use a *'rainy day'* bank account. They are simply meant to be there for any unexpected emergencies, not as our one and only supply of resources.

However, the longer we remain in this heightened state of stress, the faster our body-mind system falls into a depressed state. Simply because we're not allowing our body-mind system the time it requires to replenish and rejuvenate itself.

We're quite literally hindering the very *building blocks* (our cells) which make up our entire system. We also stop many of the vital, health-giving processes from functioning correctly or to their optimal levels.

How do we know if we're currently living in the *Emergency Stress Mode*?

Well, are you experiencing any of the following?

• Irritability

- Low or no energy
- Teary or constant unexplained crying episodes
- Outbursts of anger
- Incapable of reasoning
- Always feel on edge
- Feel constantly stressed
- Compromised immune system
- Can't shake excess weight (no matter how much you exercise)
- Inability to concentrate or focus
- Unable to maintain relationships
- Inability to make decisions
- Want to hide from the world or *'stay under the duvet'*
- Feel overwhelmed
- Normal *day-to-day* tasks seem difficult or impossible
- Low self-esteem
- Lack of co-ordination
- Have cravings or regularly partake in *'binge'* eating
- Feel clumsy or accident prone
- Feel unable to cope with life
- Lack creativity
- Feel inadequate, weak or hopeless

If you nodded *'yes'* to more than one of the above experiences, you can pretty much guarantee, like most of modern day society, you're unknowingly living in opposition to your internal Basic Rest - Activity Cycle (BRAC). This has resulted in your body-mind system becoming depressed and depleted of many vital, health-giving chemicals, hormones, nutrients, etc.

In other words, you're attempting to operate at full power with little or no internal fuel.

Do you want to hear the great news?

You can rapidly turn this around. That's right! In no time at all, you can transform your internal body-mind system into being healthy and strong (mentally, emotionally and physically) and **working for you once again!**

In fact, you're already aware of the solution. In the very same way, we allow time for our mobile devices to recharge, or our vehicles to be re-fueled, we must allow our body-mind system *(which is infinitely more complex and intelligent)* the same privilege of time to replenish and recharge our internal batteries. **It only takes 20 minutes.**

From today, start to consciously arrange your day (as best you can) around a 1.5 - 2 hours of activity versus 20 minutes of rest schedule. This will help bring you into alignment with your internal BRAC timetable. The faster we work in alignment with our personal BRAC rhythm, the faster we can lift ourselves out of a depressed state.

Rapidly Transform Your Entire Body-Mind System
By Working In Alignment With Your BRAC

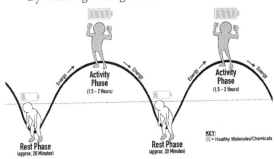

But, how do we recognise when our internal 20-minute Rest Phase is occurring, so we know when to take a vital Rest + Replenishment Break?

Signs Your Body Requires A Rest + Replenishment Break

- Become restless, fidgety, can't get comfortable and need to move around
- Feel like stretching your body (example; stretching your arms upwards toward the sky)
- Begin yawning or sighing repeatedly
- Daydreaming, fantasizing or *'drifting off'*
- Feeling a bit *'spaced out'*
- Diminished attention span, feel distracted
- Feel like having a snack or experiencing hunger pangs
- Recalling happy memories
- Feeling introspective, wanting to turn *'inward'*
- See and/or feel performance slowing down
- Feel depressed or emotionally vulnerable
- Find yourself procrastinating
- Feel like you can't continue what you're doing
- Need to urinate
- Poor concentration, inability to focus

When you become aware of one or more of the above signs, recognise this is your body's way of letting you know it's diving into the *Rest Phase* of the Basic Rest - Activity Cycle (BRAC).

Your system is literally speaking to you and saying, *'please switch off so I can rapidly refuel, replenish and rejuvenate your system to keep you running on all cylinders. It's my only way to keep you healthy and strong, mentally, emotionally and physically. It'll only take me around 20 minutes, then you'll be charged-up for the next couple of hours.'*

Remember, our entire system and fundamental processes within our body-mind system rely on the BRAC timetable.

Therefore, taking a *Rest + Replenishment Break* <u>in alignment with</u> the Rest Phase of the BRAC, ensures the vital processes within your Body-Mind system can be completed with ease. It ensures your Autonomic Nervous System, Endocrine System, Immune System, Circulatory System, Lymphatic System and all mental processes can function to the best of their abilities.

The instant you recognise any of the *'Rest + Replenishment Break'* signs, complete the simple, action steps below.

Your Rest + Replenishment Break Action Steps

1. Welcome any of the previously mentioned *Rest + Replenishment Break* signs with open arms.

2. Recognise your body-mind system is diving into a Rest Phase (to prepare you for the next Activity Phase within the Basic Rest - Activity Cycle).

3. Remove yourself (as best you can) from any external stimuli. Allow yourself to shut down ALL devices and retreat to a quiet, relaxing environment. For example: shut your office doors or walk in a quiet outdoors location. You want to eliminate as much stimuli from your environment as possible, so your body-mind system can *recharge* without interruption. Unplug from your *external world* and plug into your

internal world for restoration, invigoration and rejuvenation (approximately 20 minutes).

NOTE: If you struggle to naturally quieten your mind or switch off from the outside world, then I highly recommend you try using our **Rapidly De-Stress + Unwind Guided Meditation** which is available in our online store. If you are overly stressed, have a hard-time unwinding, struggle with *'taking time'* for yourself, or have *'worries'* you struggle to let go of, then the **Rapidly De-Stress + Unwind Guided Meditation** is right for you! You can find direct links to all our available meditations from the Main Menu at CreateADepressionFreeLife.com.

SIX ADDITIONAL HELPFUL TIPS

1. If you're aware your body is going into a Rest Phase but you're overwhelmed by the amount of work you still need to complete before a specific deadline and you therefore, feel like you can't afford to take a vital replenishment break, remind yourself: That any tasks, phone calls, texts, emails, Facebook messages, tweets, etc., can wait until later, your body-mind system cannot! *NOTE: You'll be better equipped to deal with the emails, phone calls or tasks when you return, simply because you'll be running on 'all cylinders' and be back at the peak of your game once again.* **The key is to help your body out, so it helps you out.**

2. Learning to tune in and listen to our body can take time. The more we look out for the Rest + Replenishment Break signs, the more rapidly we'll see them. So, take your time and be patient.

3. If you struggle to exercise your way out of depression, don't worry. Understand your body is depleted, drained and de-pressed. Therefore, it

111

requires rest and <u>not</u> the additional stress on your system which intense exercise can bring. **Work with your system, not against it.** Give yourself permission to rest and relax, as your body-mind system requires it to heal and repair your entire system.

4. Although the BRAC consists of a *Rest Phase* which is approximately 20 minutes in duration and an *Activity Phase* which lasts around 1.5 - 2 hours, it's not a strict *'to-the-second'* cycle we follow like a drill sergeant (it's a guideline). Everybody's internal BRAC rhythm is individual. Therefore, you must listen to your body to discover your own personal rhythm. For example:

   ♦ One person's BRAC: Rest Phase = 15 minutes and their Activity Phase = 1.5 hours.

   ♦ Another person's BRAC: Rest Phase = 25 minutes and their Activity Phase = 2 hours and 11 minutes.

5. The key is to <u>listen to your body</u> and hear what it's saying to you. The faster we tap into our personal Basic Rest - Activity Cycle, the faster we'll boost our mental, emotional and physical health and well-being. Simply because we'll be allowing our body-mind's vital internal processes to function to the best of their abilities.

6. Although the BRAC is a constant rhythm throughout our days, <u>our days are not constant</u>. Therefore, if we have a particularly stressful, intense or draining day (mentally, emotionally, or

physically), we will require longer *Rest +
Replenishment Breaks* (more than 20 minutes) to
compensate for this *'tax'* upon our system.

Still struggle to find time for essential Rest +
Replenishment Breaks?

When you feel, your system is moving into a natural
Rest Phase and you're unable to refrain from working or
you cannot get away from your desk, you can help your
system out by avoiding any high intensity, focussed,
mentally-demanding, or highly technical activities for
the next half hour or so. Only complete the simplest of
tasks (for example, mind numbing tasks, or ones that
require little or no effort), whilst your system is in this
Rest Phase.

This **does not** replace a complete Rest +
Replenishment Break. However, it does take the *pressure
off* your body-mind system, whilst it's in this Rest Phase.
This will allow your system to complete many of the
essential *'behind the scenes'* maintenance and housekeeping
duties, to keep you functioning throughout your day.

WARNING

If we choose to miss our essential Rest +
Replenishment breaks after becoming aware of the
Basic Rest - Activity Cycle, which governs our entire
body-mind system, then it's at our own peril.

We cannot grumble or complain when our system
breaks down, becomes clumsy, aggressive, overly
emotionally, depressed or mentally exhausted because
the keys to our own health and well-being are firmly
placed within our own hands.

At the end of the day, we only have two options:

1. We learn to make time for essential *Rest + Replenishment Breaks* throughout our day, working in alignment with our internal BRAC to ensure we remain in peak mental, emotional and physical condition. Or,

2. We will be FORCED to make time when our body-mind system breaks down (mentally, emotionally, and physically), interrupting our lives and destroying our schedule completely. Simply because we refuse to work in alignment with our BRAC (which controls everything from cell division to sexual arousal, from our energy levels to our emotional well-being, from our organ function to our digestion).

One option, keeps us in a **peak state of health**. The other, keeps us in a **peak state of stress**.

The ultimate choice is ours, but one way or another, **we will** have to find the time to rest.

We Are 100% Responsible For Our Own Health And Well-Being

SECTION 3

PRACTICAL RESOURCES:
Transform Your Emotions And Your Life

15

DON'T JUST PRUNE THE LEAVES!

For you to receive the greatest benefits from the extremely valuable techniques held within the pages of this Resources Section, we need to take a few moments now to delve deeper into two of the most common symptoms associated with depression, which are:

1. An abundance of anger or aggression
2. Constant, uncontrollable crying or sadness

Now, have you ever started crying immediately after being angry? Or, experienced anger in times of grief or great sadness?

Well, whether we're aware of it or not, anger and sadness are in fact the very same energy.

Yes. That's right! The very same energy and just like a pendulum swings from left to right, sadness can rapidly turn into anger and anger into sadness. They are two sides of the same coin.

- Sadness is a *passive* form of anger
- Anger is an *active* form of sadness

To understand this clearer and therefore, help elevate you out of depression, let's imagine a see-saw with sadness on one end and anger on the other.

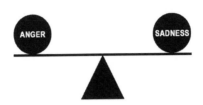

Now, if one emotion becomes heavier it will naturally *de-press* that end of the see-saw, causing the other emotion to naturally rise to the surface.

Be aware, it's the emotion we've been forcing down and *de-pressing*, that's the *underlying driver of our de-pression*. Not the one being expressed on the surface. The expressed emotion is merely a reflection, of what's being de-pressed beneath the surface.

This is the very reason depression is never treated correctly.

Simply because the usual treatments are trying to fix our expressed (surface level) emotion; our crying or our angry outbursts. However, what we're expressing to the world is NOT the core of the issue. The de-pressed emotion is. It's not called *de-pression* for nothing! We are quite literally *de-pressing* the heart of the issue.

Therefore, if you're <u>experiencing great anger</u> in depression, what sadness are you burying? Is there any grief that you haven't let go of? Are there tears you're holding back? Is there something upsetting you that you don't wish to acknowledge?

Anger Is The Result Of De-pressed (Buried) Sadness

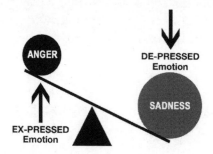

On the other hand, if you're <u>experiencing great sadness</u> in depression, is there something you're frustrated or angry about but you're struggling to process or express? Are your boundaries constantly being broken or challenged, yet you won't speak up? Do you have pent up anger you're not expressing in a constructive way?

Sadness Is The Result Of De-pressed (Buried) Anger

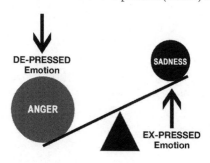

Once we're aware of this very natural relationship between sadness and anger, it's easy to see why people usually experience recurring bouts of depression.

This is because if we don't deal with the *root cause* of the issue (the de-pressed emotion/s), it'll simply grow back like a tree, again and again.

Unfortunately, this is exactly what most usual depression treatments are attempting to do. They're trying to destroy the tree by simply pruning the leaves. It's never going to happen.

So, if you've finally had enough of smacking your head against a brick wall and getting nowhere with superficial *'leaf pruning'* treatments, then the first step you need to take, is to start being honest with yourself and begin looking deeper into your feelings and responses to situations.

For example, if you're experiencing great sadness, ask yourself why?

Now, don't be tempted to accept the first answer that comes to mind. Dig a little deeper. Find those *'roots'* of your sadness which are buried deep within anger or frustration.

Just for a moment, let's imagine we feel sad and abandoned by our partner, who recently walked out on us. Sadness is what we express to the world.

However, if we look deeper and venture beneath the surface, we'll begin to discover that we have a great deal of natural anger and hostility attached to the event. We feel betrayed, let down and thrown aside.

These deep-seated emotions are the ones driving our greatest pain. Not our sadness which is on the surface.

We must be aware, that to not only get out, but stay out of depression, we're required to embrace all parts of an emotion. The passive and active sides. Which means, we must not de-press any side of the *Anger/Sadness See-Saw* or we'll continue to feel lopsided and leave ourselves open for de-pression.

We Must Heal The De-pressed Emotion To Dissolve Depression

From today, start looking deeper into what's behind your expressed emotions.

If you have great sadness, look deeper to discover where anger resides within you. If you're displaying anger, dig deeper to reveal where a great sadness lies within.

NOTE: If you feel that an event or trauma has ruined your life, or been the cause of your depression, let me share a secret with you.

In my younger years, I was assaulted by a doctor. Now, many would say this event contributed to my depression. Could that be true?

Well, I used to think so.

However, in all honesty, the answer is no. *It was never the event that caused depression but the burying (de-pression) of my sadness and anger surrounding it.*

I never dealt with all the powerful emotions that came up during that period of my life. Also, since I'm a

121

naturally aggressive personality, I thought the *right thing* to do was to de-press and bury my emotions.

I believed, if I simply stayed strong and kept moving, all would be well and I could continue moving forward with my life.

How wrong was I?!

Truth was, I didn't know any other way to cope back then. I simply wasn't equipped with the skills or knowledge to process what I'd been through. So, I did what I thought was best; bury (de-press) my emotions and keep running.

That is one of the greatest paradoxes of life.

We do not have the necessary experience until <u>after</u> we've been through, the very situation we needed it for.

The valuable lesson I can pass on to you from my very own painful experience, is to never leave the conclusion of your feelings at the victim level.

What do I mean by that?

Never allow yourself to become a victim of the *'blame game,'* and yes, that's easier said than done sometimes. But it's the only way we can bring the power and energy back into ourselves to heal.

We must delve deeper than the natural thought processes of, *'my life is cr*p because of such and such event,'* or *'I wouldn't be like this if it wasn't for that or them.'*

Yes. We are right!

We wouldn't be who we are right now, if those people or that event never occurred in our life, but it did. So, we must take courage and strength in the fact, that the event was given to us to uncover our strength in adversity.

You never know how strong you are, until being strong is your only choice.

~ Bob Marley ~

Ask yourself, does a tiny seed seem like it *should* be able to survive buried beneath tremendous amounts of soil and darkness?

It seems mighty illogical, that something so seemingly fragile could sustain such things.

However, this seed will **not** sprout, will **not** become all that it was meant to become, will **not** break into the light, will **not** discover its fullest potential **without** being placed under this vast amount of pressure and darkness.

You are no different.

Just like a tiny seed, life doesn't give you anything that you cannot handle. Life knows you have the strength to get through it, and get through it you will.

Remember, unless we have some adversity in our lives, we'll never be able to see what we're truly capable of and you have far, far more strength inside of you, than you're currently aware of.

Naturally, I'm completely unaware of what challenges you must face in your life but understand this; no matter what you're currently going through, once you face it head on, **you'll unlock an unbreakable strength inside of you**. A strength which can never be taken away from you.

In fact, after everything I've been through, I've come to recognise that the seemingly *'low points'* in our lives, are merely **spring boards to much greater heights**.

Think about it, the lower the spring board goes, the greater heights we can reach.

After all, the spring board MUST bounce back the same distance, in the opposite direction. That's the laws of physics and ultimately, the laws of the universe.

Remember, no matter how deep you're in it or how bad you think it is, you can get out of de-pression.

Do NOT let de-pression define who you are.

De-pression is NOT who you are.

Who you are, is hidden behind de-pressed energy, emotions and all those societal layers which are keeping the exquisite *Masterpiece of You* locked in darkness.

Make the commitment to yourself today to get out of de-pression, by integrating one or more of the following techniques into your daily life.

You'll be glad you did!

I look forward to seeing you in the following pages...

16

EXPERIENCING GREAT SADNESS?

(NOTE: Because anger/sadness are the same energy, you may need to rotate between this technique and the one dedicated to anger in the next chapter. Use the technique that feels right for you).

I recommend you complete this technique for 3 consecutive days initially. After this initial period, use this technique anytime you feel sadness arise within you.

To begin, go somewhere private where you'll not be disturbed.

If you haven't got the feeling of sadness already, imagine a time when you were very upset or sad (this isn't usually difficult when we're depressed).

Now sit silently and let your sadness come up. DO NOT withhold anything or attempt to stop your sadness or tears. Just allow the feelings to rise, allow them to bubble up to the surface and flow out of you.

The important key to this technique is to NOT avoid your sadness. After all, that's exactly what has got us into de-pression in the first place: Avoidance. We've been de-pressing our authentic thoughts and feelings, in an attempt, to avoid them (whether consciously or not).

Therefore, if we ever want out of de-pression, we must give ourselves the *permission to feel* whatever we feel without judgement.

Sadness is a natural emotion, a natural feeling. It's a human emotion. There's no way to avoid it in life and be aware, the sooner we allow the energy to flow, the sooner it will go. It's the law of nature; the ebb and flow cycle of life.

Throughout this technique DO NOT stem the flow of your tears, just allow them to flow naturally. Let your whole body feel your tears and let every cell in your body cry, just let it flow and let it out.

The Advanced Secret

A highly transformative master step which can easily be added to this technique, is when you feel completely emptied of tears, imagine something that makes you feel sad all over again and let your sadness come up *again* and cry even more.

Allow, *even more* tears to flow out of your system. I promise, you'll be surprised just how much sadness you have unknowingly locked away inside you all these years.

After completing this technique correctly, you'll instantly reside in a calm, quiet and still place. You'll feel lighter, fresher and clearer than you've ever felt before.

This technique is exactly what I did and I cannot recommend it enough.

After completing this exercise in the depths of depression, it was the first time, I felt light, I felt peaceful and I felt calm. I couldn't believe it! All by using the very tears I had bubbling up nearly every moment of every day.

So, don't delay, give it a go for yourself today!

Why is this technique so powerful in transforming depression?

Not only does this technique work directly with the energy involved in depression, but it also works with the emotion of sadness and sadness is an extremely powerful and transformative energy, if we use it correctly and to our advantage.

If used wisely, sadness can cleanse our soul in the same way, a storm cleanses the air.

The unfortunate truth is, most of us spend our entire lives trying to escape sadness or avoid our innate feelings of loneliness but depression fair *'slaps us'* in the face. We have no place left to hide anymore, we can no longer run away from our authentic feelings.

It's as if we're being forced to confront our loneliness and sadness all at once, whether we like it or not.

Therefore, we need to understand what a valuable moment we've been given.

In all honesty, we may not like the pain that's associated with depression. We may believe it's the worst time in our life. However, what we're NOT seeing, is that we've been given a chance to surpass the fear of our loneliness, the fear of sadness. We've been given a chance to surpass the mediocre and go where others spend their whole lives fearing to tread.

Remember, life trusts that a fragile seed <u>WILL</u> break out of the darkness and emerge as a mighty oak, powerful, grand and strong. Life also trusts that YOU have the potential, just like that tiny seed, to *break through the darkness* it throws upon you and reach for the stars.

So, when you sit back and think about it, with life and the whole of existence backing you to get through this, you simply cannot lose!

IMPORTANT NOTE

I'll be honest with you, when I completed this technique for the very first time, it felt intense. I was curled up on the floor of my apartment and every cell of my body felt like it was in sheer agony from crying so much. You must not be afraid. Remember, it's simply a purification process, where we are releasing and eliminating all that pent-up energy of sadness that's been de-pressed within our system for so many years. Therefore, it's naturally going to feel uncomfortable at times.

In those times, remember the fact that once a volcano has erupted, it's calm again. That's all we're doing here, we're *releasing the cork* and setting the energy free, in a controlled and safe manner.

We're also mastering the *'advanced art'* of turning the cards we've been dealt into our favour by **using our very de-pression to literally catapult us up and out of depression**.

So, begin using this technique today, and continue it for at least 3 consecutive days, depending upon your depth of sadness.

17

EXPERIENCING GREAT ANGER?

(NOTE: Because anger/sadness are the same energy, you may need to rotate between this technique and the one dedicated to sadness in the previous chapter. Use the technique that feels right for you).

I recommend you complete this technique for 3 consecutive days initially. After this initial period, use this technique anytime you feel anger arise within you.

First, I'll explain the technique. Then, I'll explain the how and why this technique works so well and why it's vital in helping catapult us out of depression.

If you haven't already got the feeling of anger, simply imagine a time when you felt angry or betrayed.

If that's a struggle, simply imagine a situation, event or person that drives you crazy or irritates you. I'm sure we all have at least a handful of those to choose from in our lives. It doesn't need to be recent, just remember it and feel your anger rise. Then, complete the following technique for approximately 20 minutes or so. (Note: The more often we complete this exercise, the shorter the timespan required).

Go somewhere private and allow your anger to rise.

Remember it's just energy, nothing sinister or wrong is happening. So, DO NOT withhold anything or even attempt to prevent your anger.

You want to get it up and out of your system as fast as possible, so just release it. Not *at* anyone and only, in a safe and controlled manner.

So, how do release the energy of anger safely?

We need to do something *active* to get anger out of our system, to loosen its grip on us. This is because anger is an active emotion. Anger drives us. It gives us steam.

So, you need to either scream, jump, yell, punch or kick the air, do whatever your body feels like doing to release the steam from your system.

Now, if we feel particularly violent in any way or we have an urge to kill, then kill a boxing bag. If you don't have one of those, then kill a pillow instead. Punch it, kick it, bite it, throw it, drop-kick it to the other side of the universe if you want to. Just get all that anger up and out of your system.

If you feel great anger towards someone, imagine their face on that pillow (just don't tell them afterwards) and continue to beat that pillow up.

Alternatively, if you can be outside (and remain safe), kick the stuffing out of a ball against a wall.

Whichever way you decide to drive the energy of anger up and out of your system, throw your whole body into this technique.

If you do this correctly, then every part of your being will start to feel intense and alive. Go with it and DO NOT withhold anything.

Remember, you want that energy up and out of your system, so let it all out in a safe and controlled environment.

After doing this technique a few times you'll notice, that you'll become calmer throughout your days, and whilst working directly with your anger, you will have also worked with the same energy that can turn into sadness if de-pressed. It's like killing two birds with one stone. That's greater results with less effort!

Misunderstanding Anger

Now, a great majority of people are afraid of anger. There is a great fear that once unleashed, like some wild beast, it'll be untameable, it'll take control of us and we'll be lost forever.

Therefore, I'd like to take a few moments to explain the energy of anger in much greater detail so you'll have more clarity of its true nature.

(Note: If you're aware that you have a great fear of anger, this technique is going to be most beneficial for you to complete. After all, if you're afraid of the energy of anger, you've most definitely de-pressed it throughout your life).

The True Essence of Anger

Can you remember as a child, being dressed in clothing or shoes by your parents that you thought were absolutely disgusting, ugly or just down right embarrassing?

Maybe you had to wear a particular outfit on special occasions and you hated every second of it. You didn't want to wear it but you were forced to. You know that feeling, right?

It's that feeling, when you can't wait to get home so you can rip off those ugly clothes and jump into something more comfortable. Something that makes you feel more like *'you.'*

Well, this anger technique is the same process. Anger is a *'layer'* of energy; exactly like a *'layer'* of clothing.

Just like those awful clothes our parents made us wear, <u>anger is not and has never been</u> a representation of who we are as a person.

It's simply, a temporary *'suit'* we've been wearing.

So, imagine releasing yourself from the energy of anger, in the exact same way you would release yourself from all those layers of clothing you were forced to wear as a child.

**Anger is not who you are! So, just throw it off!
Release it!**

<u>IMPORTANT NOTES + WARNINGS</u>

- You may feel insane, stupid, foolish, loony or even nasty or bad at any time during this technique. Don't worry. This is reason I recommend you complete this technique in a private location. A location in which you are free from judgements and free from hurting others and/or yourself.

- Be aware, no one is free from this energy. Absolutely no one. Not even your so-called saints. So, do not believe for one second, that you have to release this energy of anger because you are somehow mental or a bad person. Everyone has this energy inside of them, it's how we are all created.

- I do not want anybody to misunderstand me in any way. **I do NOT condone violence towards anyone** (including ourselves) or anything else for that matter (other than the pillow, boxing bag or ball I mentioned earlier). Keep yourself, others and any other living creatures safe from harm AT ALL TIMES. Also, I know I don't need to mention it but I will for the record, it's never okay to damage another person's property.

- Be aware that we must release the energy of anger in a physical, active form but never put yourself and/or others in any danger throughout this technique.

- If you choose to complete this technique outside, you must make sure you cannot be harmed, by others and/or vehicles. Take complete responsibility for your safety and the safety of others, at all times.

- Last, but not least, enter this technique with light heartedness, it's fun, it's refreshing. You will feel energised afterwards and of course, you'll help lift that heavy energy which is keeping you stuck in a state of de-pression. Enjoy!

18

THE INSTANT TRANQUILLIZER AND RAPID DE-STRESS TECHNIQUE

This technique can be repeated as often as necessary throughout your day. After completing, you can expect to feel calm and tranquil.

This technique is nature's instant tranquillizer for the body, mind and spirit.

It's also highly beneficial for relieving headaches.

Sit in a relaxed position with your back straight. Close your eyes and take a slow, deep breath in and out. Feel yourself slowly unwind and relax, then complete the following steps.

1. Place your right hand in front of you and fold your index and middle fingers inwards.

2. Whilst maintaining this hand position (as best you can), press your right nostril closed with your right thumb and inhale slowly and quietly through your left nostril to a count of 8 (or less, if required). Figure A.

Figure A

3. Now place your pinky and ring fingers onto your left nostril (whilst still holding the right closed) and retain the air for a count of 8 (or less, if required). Figure B.

Figure B

4. Then lift your thumb, releasing the right nostril (whilst still holding the left closed) and exhale slowly and quietly through the right nostril (count of 8 or less, if required). Figure C.

Figure C

5. Whilst your hand remains in this position (Figure C), slowly inhale through your right nostril to a count of 8 (or the same count you're using throughout this entire technique).

6. Place your thumb onto your right nostril (whilst still holding the left closed) and retain the air for a count of 8 (or usual count). Figure D.

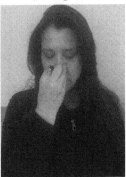

Figure D

7. Then lift your pinky and ring fingers, releasing the left nostril (whilst still holding the right closed) and exhale slowly and quietly through the left nostril (count of 8 or less, if required). Figure E.

Figure E

8. Now you have returned to the starting position. Repeat steps 2 - 7 another 6 times to make a total of 7.

At no point during this technique should you force or stress your body. Be gentle and only use a count throughout the entire routine, which is comfortable for you. For example: If you struggle to retain the breath for a count of 8, no worries! Simply try holding for a count of 3 or 4 to begin with and work towards 8.

Work with what feels right for you and remember, the most important thing is not the count but that you complete this simple technique so you can receive the tremendous benefits.

After completing this *instant tranquillizer*, you will feel calm, de-stressed, internally strengthened and centred.

19

11 MINUTES TO INNER CALM AND TRANQUILITY

This simple technique instantly creates a *'gateway'* into your inner silence, inner beauty and inner calm and who in their right mind doesn't like the sound of that?

This technique can be used anytime you feel the need to **escape from the world** and **recharge your batteries**. It's also highly beneficial if you suffer from insomnia.

The Technique

Simply sit or lie in a comfortable position, close your eyes and become aware of your breath. Take a few deep breaths, in and out, and feel yourself slow down and relax.

Now become aware of how your body feels. Starting from your feet and working upwards, scan your whole body, bit by bit.

Is there any part of your body which is tense?

If so, increase the tension by tensing that part of your body as much as possible, then suddenly relax it.

Pay particular attention to your facial muscles, as they carry 90% of your tensions. This is because our minds are the source of many tensions within our lives. Therefore, our face becomes the *storage place* for these tensions.

So, when scanning your body, screw up your face as much as possible and then suddenly relax it.

Do this for all parts of your body until you can scan it and it feels completely relaxed.

With your eyes still closed, bring your attention to the area of your chest between your armpits, your heart area and totally forget the rest of your body.

Now, once all your awareness is on your heart area, feel this area fill with great peace and gratitude. If it helps, you can visualise a peaceful scene within this area of your chest.

What type of scenes evoke feelings of peace, gratefulness and calm within you? (A waterfall? A meandering river? A child smiling? An embrace?)

Whatever scene it is, simply imagine it playing out within your heart area.

As the scene unfolds, you will begin to feel a greater sense of peacefulness wash over you. Stay with this feeling, bathe in it and feel it expand in all directions until it completely surrounds you, in its tranquil, calming radiance.

Bathe in this feeling for at least 11 minutes (or longer, if you prefer).

Now, when you feel ready, gently open your eyes and continue your day feeling more calm and relaxed.

That's it!

11 minutes to relaxation and inner calm.

Don't believe it's that easy?

No worries! Give it a go and see and feel the difference in yourself.

This technique is most beneficial when completed immediately after waking, or before going to sleep.

20

EXPERIENCE THE 'GAP'

The following technique is about simply observing your emotions.

This technique helps you work with any feeling which comes up throughout depression, or throughout your life in general.

Complete this technique as often as you like, especially when you're experiencing challenging or strong emotions.

Sit comfortably, close your eyes and take 7 deep breaths and stay with the emotion that you're currently feeling.

Simply shift from *thinking* about it, to *feeling* the sensations within your body. Feel what's happening inside of you when you're feeling such emotions as: sadness, anger, rage, fear, jealousy, etc.

Depending upon the emotion you're currently experiencing, you may feel like tensing up your body or fear may arise. That's okay, just take another 7 deep breaths and know that you'll be fine and continue to *feel the sensations*.

Feel yourself relax into your body, with every breath you take.

As you relax, you will observe that your emotions naturally subside or transform into a different feeling. They do not stay. They come and they go.

Just observe your emotions and the sensations within your body. Remember, nothing will harm you.

Emotions are merely *waves of energy*, or energy in motion (e-motions). Therefore, if we allow the wave to flow naturally, it will subside without any interference.

Continue this exercise until you feel the natural transformation within your emotions. Begin to recognise, **you are not your emotions**. See them as visitors that come and go.

What this technique allows you to do is create a *'gap.'* A gap, between you and your emotions. After all, if YOU are observing your emotions, then YOU cannot be them. You cannot watch them and be them at the same time, just like you cannot observe your own face (without external aids).

Once you experience this *gap*, this separateness, between yourself and emotions, you will naturally experience a massive shift in your depression.

Alternative Method

Depending upon our personality we may require a different approach to our emotions than the previously described method.

So, here's an effective variation of this technique.

We begin the technique as described previously, however, we add a very powerful twist to it.

142

Instead of simply observing the emotion, we *'own'* the e-motion.

Now, what do I mean by that?

Well, whilst experiencing any emotion, we say out loud:

'I am (the emotion)'

For example:

- If I'm experiencing anger, then to *'own'* it, I would say, *'I am anger.'*
- If I'm experiencing great fear, I would say out loud, *'I am fear.'*
- If I'm feeling sad, I say, *'I am sadness.'*

TAKE NOTE: I do not say, I am an<u>gry</u>. Which is what we usually say when we experience great anger. Instead, I say, I am an<u>ger</u>. I don't say, I am sad. I say, I am sad-ness. **We are expressing the actual emotion**.

This is a very powerful technique because it instantly transforms the energy of the e-motion.

This instant change occurs because once we acknowledge something or shine a light onto it, it cannot hide anymore.

More to the point, we're not trying to hide it or push it aside. We're not trying to subdue, de-press or change the e-motion in any way. And, just like a child when given attention, it naturally calms down.

When we relax, and observe the feelings within our body, we'll begin to see that our e-motions are no different than the tides of the ocean. They are forever in motion.

No matter what e-motion we may be having, it will pass.

So, relax, breathe and just observe without labelling any emotion as good or bad. All emotions are necessary for us to experience all the richness life has to offer.

Use this technique as often as you can to free yourself from the belief that you are your emotions. You are not. You are separate from them and you are exquisite!

21

HAPPINESS STARTS WITH AN INNER SMILE

You'll want to complete this technique as often as you can because the results are instant!

Do it anytime, anywhere (except whilst walking, driving or operating heavy machinery).

Close your eyes, sit comfortably and start breathing gently through your nose. Just allow your body to breathe naturally, do not force anything.

After you feel your body has slowed down and become more relaxed, start feeling a smile, except <u>NOT</u> on your face but in your belly.

Visualise your belly smiling inside.

Now, there's no need to smile on your face, but if you do, then just allow it to happen naturally.

As you continue to visualise your belly smiling inside, you'll begin to feel the energy permeate across your whole body, just allow it and enjoy it.

Anytime you feel happiness is missing, simply close your eyes, relax and see your inner smile within your belly once again.

Your *inner smile* is always there, so you can reconnect with it anytime you like.

This technique connects you with your true inner being, your true inner self that's intrinsically full of happiness, that's why it's so very effective.

NOTE: Don't be fooled by its simplicity. Don't delay, give it a go now!

Alternatively, instead of *going it alone* you can listen to the relaxing **Unlock Your Inner Smile + Authentic Happiness Guided Meditation** which is available in our online store. If you struggle to feel any real, authentic happiness in your life, or you want to discover the secret to tapping into the *'inner well'* of happiness which resides within you 24/7, then the **Unlock Your Inner Smile + Authentic Happiness Guided Meditation** is right for you! You can find direct links to all our available meditations from the Main Menu at CreateADepressionFreeLife.com.

22

JUST SAY YES!

When you get up in the morning simply say *'YES'* at least 12 times (or anytime you have nothing to do). There's no need to find something to say *'yes to,'* just say the word YES out loud.

Seriously, that's it! Simple, isn't it?

You don't even need any enthusiasm when you do this technique, that's because the word YES will instantly improve and uplift your energy naturally.

Whether we're aware of it or not, the word YES naturally opens up our energy, making it vibrate more positively and making us more receptive to life and since like attracts like, the more positive we can make our energy, the more positive our environments will become.

Yes and no are not just words, but doors!

Do you remember a time when you were excited to share something with someone, ask them to go somewhere with you, or ask someone if you could go somewhere? You were all excited because you couldn't wait to do whatever it was you were looking forward to doing, but then the other person slaps you with a big fat 'NO!'

You know that feeling, right?

Well, that NO, closes our energy system. We shut ourselves down and we feel awful.

Now, this is a very natural response because our system believes the other person is against us. Therefore, our energy goes into a type of *protective mode*.

At first, this isn't an issue. However, a problem occurs if we stay in this *protective mode* for far too long. It becomes a way of life. We become unhealthy and often, de-pressed. After all, we're de-pressing what we truly feel and we're de-pressing our natural enthusiasm.

The World of No

For a moment, imagine yourself standing inside your home with all the doors, windows and drapes shut tight. You may feel safe and protected inside the house because all the *perceived dangers* have been locked outside, but so has everything else.

Absolutely nothing can enter your home.

- No opportunities.
- No new possibilities.
- No new ideas.
- No new people.

You become stuck inside a closed house. This is what the *'World of No'* looks like from an energy perspective.

In the midst of depression we need newness, we need new possibilities, new opportunities and new ways of living and the only way to allow the new to enter, is for us to open our doors and allow in some light and that's what the word 'YES' does to our energy system.

It opens us up to new possibilities and who in their right mind doesn't like that idea?

Now, if you don't believe me that simply saying the word 'YES' can be so beneficial, that's okay. Give it a go and find out for yourself.

Trust me, you might be surprised what a little bit of YES can do for your life.

Repeat the word YES several times right now! Go on! I dare you. Scream YES, as loud as you can!

YES!

SECTION 4

CREATE YOUR
DEPRESSION-FREE FUTURE

23

YOUR DEPRESSION-FREE LIFE REQUIRES ATTENTION

"Everything in this universe consists of energy. Your home, your car, you, me, we're all comprised of the same thing; energy. The only difference between you and a house, or me and a car, is the rate of vibration or frequency at which this energy vibrates."

To rapidly create a depression-free life, we don't need anymore, airy-fairy, self-help, positive thinking books. Instead, we need to time-travel back to 1841 and shake hands with the German physicist and physician Julius Robert von Mayer (one of the founding fathers of thermodynamics) and thank him for declaring that, *'energy is neither created nor destroyed.'*

This means that the VERY energy needed to create anything you desire in your life is already in existence around you.

It must be!

Since, energy can neither be created nor destroyed, only transformed from one form to another.

153

Which is exciting news, if we want to create a depression-free future and rapidly transform our lives!

But first, we must delve one level deeper into the realm of science to truly understand the *depression-crushing* capabilities of this scientific law; energy is neither created nor destroyed.

Now, if you're a person who never enjoyed science at school, please bear with me here because once you understand the truth about what happens in the world around you, you'll begin to see how to rapidly transform your life using proven scientific methods.

So, let's get started.

Firstly, we need to be aware that energy comes in two forms:

1. **A Wave:** Waves are *formless* energy. In other words, the energy has not taken *'shape'* or *'form'* yet. Which means, waves are full of limitless possibilities.

2. **A Particle:** Particles are *formed* energy. They've started to materialise and *form* into something solid. Which means, the limitless possibilities associated with the wave are no longer available.

Now, what in the world have scientific discussions about particles and waves, got to do with getting out of depression?

More than you know!

In fact, what you're about to discover is a **must-know** if you want to accelerate your journey up and out of depression.

You see, right this very minute, wherever you are in the world, science declares there's a massive field of energy surrounding you. *A field of energy which is full of waves of limitless possibilities.*

Yes! Whether you're aware of it or not, your current environment is pregnant with unlimited possibilities. Everything you could ever imagine and more, is possible within this *field of energy* (including a depression-free future).

We also need to be aware that energy is an *equal opportunities employer.* Which means, there are just as many *waves* of debt and hardship, as there are *waves* of wealth and abundance. There's just as many *waves* of health, as there are *waves* of disease. Alongside, *waves* of love and happiness, there's also *waves* of sadness and loneliness.

Nothing is missing from the field of energy which currently surrounds you. Everything is open, possible and available to you.

For example, if you are in a relationship, there are *waves* of love and deeper connection, alongside *waves* of heartbreak and betrayal available to you.

So, how do you choose what type of relationship you create?

Well, the answer lies, in where you place my attention.

That's right!

You see, the moment you focus your attention on something, your attention transforms it from a *formless* wave into a *formed* particle. The energy takes form (takes shape) and begins to materialise into your physical reality.

Now, even though there are always plenty of *waves* of BOTH positive and negative scenarios available to us, at all times. For this next example, let's imagine I'm going to focus all of my attention upon everything my partner does wrong (negative waves).

Now, as you'll recall, the moment we focus on a *wave* (whether positive or negative), it becomes a *particle* and starts to take shape and materializes into our world.

Which means, the more I *'hone in on,'* or focus upon my partner's mistakes (negative waves), the relationship is going to manifest (form and take shape) into a very negative, fault-finding, conflict-riddled scenario.

Of course, I can rapidly shift my focus to grateful, appreciative *waves* which are also available to me, but they'll require time to *form* and in this example, my relationship has no time left. Simply because I've spent far too long focussing on the negative waves of possibilities between us.

The important golden nugget to remember, is the act of focusing our attention on any *wave of possibility*, causes it to become a particle and *take form*, manifesting into our physical reality.

FACT: Our Focus CREATES Our World

Ask yourself:

- Where has, your focus been placed lately?
- What types of images, TV programs, movies, etc., do you pour your attention into?
- What do you spend most of your time focussing on? Waves of gratefulness and abundance? Or waves of doubt, violence, fear and scarcity?
- More importantly, what tiny changes can you implement today, to start focussing on the more

positive aspects of your life, yourself, others, your relationship, your job, etc.?

Now, you've already learnt that the scientific greats of the 1800's discovered, *'energy can be neither created nor destroyed.'* So, if we take this wisdom and imagine a massive pool of energy, like a gigantic lake.

If energy can be neither created nor destroyed, then everything that comes into existence <u>must be</u> effectively *born* from this same giant pool of energy; you, me, the trees, our pets, our homes, the stars, cars, money, our loved ones, etc. Which means, everything you've ever wanted; you're already connected to.

Massive Pool of Energy

Everything you want to create or bring into your life is already A PART OF YOU and you are a part of it.

Just, ponder on that thought for a moment...

Now, the main reason I went all *'sciency'* on you, was not to convert you into a science graduate. It also wasn't an attempt to baffle you with science (I don't know enough to do that).

I simply wanted to illustrate (with scientific proof) that YOU CAN CREATE ANYTHING you set your mind (focus) to, because:

✓ Whatever you focus on *takes shape* in your physical world.

✓ Whatever you want *you're already connected to,* on a much deeper level.

These scientific laws are the very reason why many people struggle to get out of depression. Simply because they are placing all their attention (focus) upon depression itself and on fighting it.

However, the more attention we give something, the more energy we are pouring into it and the more it grows, **effectively making our struggle out of depression worse.**

What you resist, persists
~ Carl Jung (1875 - 1961) ~

Ironically, the very key to getting out of depression, is **not** to focus on getting out of it. Instead, it's more beneficial to shift our focus 180 degrees, by asking ourselves; what does a depression-free life look like to us?

Then, we simply *tune in* and *focus on* those positive aspects within ourselves, others and the world around us.

The key to remember, is to always focus on what you DO want, not on what you don't want. The great Socrates was aware of this great wisdom over 2,415 years ago, when he stated:

The secret of change is to focus all your energy not on fighting the old, but on building the new.
~ Socrates (circa. 470 BC - 399 BC) ~

To help you easily focus on what you truly want in life and rapidly create a depression-free future, I'm sharing **The Ultimate Day Technique**.

This technique involves a series of very simple questions which will help to instantly reveal what truly makes you *tick* as a person and what lights up your world.

After all, if there's one thing we lose touch with in the depths of depression, it's what motivates and inspires us in life.

Fortunately, *The Ultimate Day Technique* helps resolve this.

Keep in mind, when answering the following questions to not feel limited in any way. You're now aware that surrounding you right now, is *a field of energy which contains everything*.

You've also learnt that you're already connected to everything you desire to create in your life, on a very intimate level.

Truth is, whatever you wish to create is simply waiting for you to focus on it. So then, it can transform from a formless wave into a solid particle. Allowing it to form, materialise and *'take shape'* in your physical reality.

The Ultimate Day Technique

No matter how we view our life in relation to time, whether we measure it in terms of days, weeks, months, or even years, our life always comes back to being made up of a *collection of days*, doesn't it?

There are so many *'days'* in a week, in a month, in a year, in a lifetime.

Therefore, it makes sense if we're attempting to create the most uplifting and fulfilling life for ourselves, we simply need to start with one day.

That's it, just one!

Think about it, if we can create one awesome day, all we need to do is then multiply that 1 day by 365 (days) and we effortlessly create ourselves one awesome year.

1 Ultimate Day x 365 = 1 Awesome Year!

So, that's exactly what we're going to do.

Starting right now, we're going to begin creating your *Ultimate Day*.

First, place yourself in a quiet space away from others. Shut off all phones and/or distractions and write down your answers to the following questions as honestly as possible.

This technique will rapidly *bring to light* what you truly want and need in your life, in your relationships and in your working life for you to feel truly fulfilled and complete, from the inside, out.

When answering every question never feel limited by your current circumstances. Think big, be creative and always remember, there are *waves of endless possibilities* surrounding you every single moment.

Ask yourself, **if you could have the most ideal, amazing and ultimate day of your life, what would it look like?** *(Remember, think big! Then answer the following questions).*

- Where would you live on your ideal day?
  (Seaside? Mountainside? Coastal? Inland?)
- Who would you live with?
  (Family? Friends? Alone? With pets?)
- What would your home look like?
  (Apartment? Mansion? House Boat?)
- What view would you have from your home?

(Sea? Mountains? City Lights?)

- What furnishings would you have in your home?
- What time would you get up in the morning and who would you wake up with?
- What clothes would you put on in the morning and what would you be doing first thing?
- What are your first thoughts of the day?
- What would you have for breakfast, where and who with? If you're with others, what do you talk about?
- What would you spend the first half of your day doing? Working? Exercising? Relaxing? Helping others?
- If you must take children to school, what do you talk about? What would you be thinking about? What would you be driving? Or would you prefer to walk or cycle?
- Do you take the dog for a walk? Attend yoga? Go to the gym? Go shopping? Start baking? Complete a morning Sudoku/crossword? Or, simply chill out?

Break your morning down as much as possible. Describe as many details as you can and remember this is your ideal day, it doesn't necessarily reflect your present days. So, don't feel limited by your present perceived boundaries. Think *'unlimited possibilities'* and continue with the questions…

- What would you have for lunch? Who with and where?
- What about your friends? What would they be like? Seriously think about it. If you could surround yourself with any type of person in the world, what type would it be? What would they talk about? Is the conversation always inspiring and stimulating?

161

Remember, this is your ideal day, so I can't imagine you want to waste it on idle gossip, right? So, get creative!

- What would you do for personal fulfilment?
- What would your job/career be? In what way, do you contribute to others?
- What life purpose do you have? To help others? To bring joy to others? To be creative? To supply healthy food to others? What would inspire you? What purpose would cause you to wake up excited on a daily basis? Again, think big!
- Would you have a business? If so, what would it be?
- What hours would your ideal job have? Would you work alone or with others? What would you do at work? What would your clients be like? Or your employees? Or your colleagues?

Caution - Don't Be Fooled

These questions may seem futile and overly simplistic. However, what they're doing is uncovering the *'keys'* to what you really want. They're getting you to look outside of your perceived limitations and discover what excites, motivates and inspires you.

Unfortunately, so many of us don't stop and ask ourselves these very simple questions about what we want in life. We simply drudge through our days on *'autopilot'* without stopping and questioning whether what we're doing makes us happy. Then we wonder why we feel so unsatisfied, bored, de-pressed, unfulfilled and frustrated. Okay back to the questions…

- What would your relationship be like with your significant other? What would they be like? What would they do with their days? What qualities do you appreciate in them? What qualities do they appreciate in you? What would you both talk about together? In what ways, do they excite and inspire you? Are they spontaneous, or do you prefer someone more reserved and careful?

- Are there any children? What would you do with your family time? How would you spend it? What do you all talk about? What is it about the family time that you appreciate and are grateful for?
- What do you do during your afternoons?
- What would dinner time be like? Are you the cook? Or someone else? What would you eat? Who with and where? What would you talk about over dinner?
- What would you do after dinner? Where and who with?
- What time would you go to bed and dare I say it, where and who with? What would your *'happy and grateful'* thoughts be as you drop off to sleep?

After completing the above questions, read through your answers to establish a complete and detailed view of your Ultimate Day.

Then, whilst holding this image in your mind, ask yourself the final potent question: *Would you be willing to live this way, every single day of your life?*

If your answer is yes! You've answered the questions correctly. However, if your answer is no, which answers need changing to reflect your ideal day? Go back and refine your answers until you create a day, you would be willing to live every single day.

When you've finished creating your ultimate day, start making steps (even the tiniest) towards making it a reality.

In other words, what can you do today to start stepping closer to your dream life?

FACT: Your past or present situation <u>does not</u> dictate your future. Start afresh today and step into an abundant, depression-free future.

Remember, science proves you're already attached to everything you want. Which means, you can have your dreams if you so desire, so GO FOR IT!

Your Essential Companion

CREATE A DEPRESSION-FREE LIFE SHOW

Create A Depression-Free Life Show: **The Essential Companion To This Book**

In this show, you'll discover more innovative strategies to rapidly breakthrough depression and when you subscribe (it's free) to the Create A Depression-Free Life Show, you'll always have regular depression help available, at your convenience.

Discover How To Overcome Depression With An Endless Supply Of Self-Help Strategies!

Also, if you have any questions regarding depression, life, love, relationships or any other subject matter I've discussed, which you would like answered on the show, then simply visit the link below for further information.

Start listening to the Create A Depression-Free Life Show today by visiting:

http://createadepressionfreelife.com

Don't delay. Listen to the show in a way that's **most convenient for you** to start creating the life you so desire and deserve today!

ABOUT THE AUTHOR

None of us need 'fixing'. Nor do we need to be hypnotised to
believe we're a better person. We simply need to DE-hynotise
ourselves from all those beliefs, saying we're not!
~ Marie's Philosophy

Marie O'Neil is a 39-year-old Author, Speaker, Transformational Life Coach and Depression-Busting Specialist currently based in Manchester, UK.

Marie has travelled to various locations across this beautiful globe to the likes of India, Europe, Australia, New Zealand, the Americas, just to name a few, in search of answers to *'what really makes us all tick.'*

On her adventures, she's gained a wide and extremely varied range of knowledge and experience from various healing modalities/systems and insightful teachers along the way. Including but not limited to; Cognitive/Behavioural psychologies, Gestalt therapy, Organisational Behaviour, Counselling Principles and Practices, Journey therapy, Meditation, Science of the Breath, Mantras, and the list goes on…

It's this hard-won wisdom which Marie imparts in all her private sessions, online courses, workshops and books.

Connect With Marie

Facebook: @MarieONeilOfficial
Website: http://CreateADepressionFreeLife.com

Made in the USA
Columbia, SC
27 March 2022

58227424R00098